ARTIFACTS
of a '90s Kid

Humorous Musings
and Observations for
Every Millennial

Alana Hitchell

ARTIFACTS
of a '90s Kid

Humorous Musings
and Observations for
Every Millennial

Alana Hitchell

Skyhorse Publishing

Skyhorse Publishing books may be purchased in bulk at special discounts for sales promotion, corporate gifts, fund-raising, or educational purposes. Special editions can also be created to specifications. For details, contact the Special Sales Department, Skyhorse Publishing, 307 West 36th Street, 11th Floor, New York,

NY 10018 or info@skyhorsepublishing.com.

Skyhorse® and Skyhorse Publishing® are registered trademarks of Skyhorse Publishing, Inc.®, a Delaware corporation.

Visit our website at www.skyhorsepublishing.com.

10 9 8 7 6 5 4 3 2 1

Library of Congress Cataloging-in-Publication Data is available on file.

Cover design by Jane Sheppard

Cover photos by Alana Hitchell

Cover Illustration: iStockphoto

Print ISBN: 978-1-5107-1662-9

Ebook ISBN: 978-1-5107-1663-6

Printed in China

Contents

My tower of diaries.

Introduction

When I was about eight years old, I asked my mom for a diary. I wasn't sure exactly what to write about, but after years of walking into my sister's room and seeing her quickly toss the spiral notebook she was writing in under her bed, I became intrigued. After making sure my sister would be out of the house for a while, I decided to sneak a peek at her diary. I was so captivated by all the new things I was learning that reading her diary became a weekly event and motivated me to start my own.

I realized early on that when I was feeling sad or upset and my parents weren't around to complain to, I could write about how I was feeling in my diary and would wind up feeling much better. I began taking my diary everywhere I went: family functions, sleepovers, on vacation, etc. It was like an old friend I could vent to.

I would have never imagined I'd continue writing in a diary for the next twenty years. In early 2010, I decided to back everything up on my computer and painstakingly type out every single entry. Although the process took a couple of years, I had a wonderful time reminiscing and was amazed that it ended up being nearly a thousand pages. I wanted to do something with this "book" I had written, but wasn't sure exactly what.

The thought of getting my diary published crossed my mind, but I figured it was only interesting to me because it was my life—people who didn't know me probably wouldn't care to read it. Then, in 2014, I stumbled upon a Netflix documentary called *Mortified Nation*. I randomly decided to watch it, not having a clue what it was about, and can honestly say it was a major turning point in my life. It involved people reading their old diaries onstage in front of complete strangers. I was astounded at how popular this sort of thing was and it was surprising to find out that live performances were happening in cities all over the country! It proved to me that there was indeed an interest in this type of diary-style writing.

Before I began the querying process, I wanted to test the market to see if people would actually be interested in *my* diary entries. I created a blog called *My 20-Year Diary* where I post all of my diary entries online in chronological order, starting from when I was eight years old. After receiving positive feedback, the rest is history— *Artifacts of a '90s Kid* was born.

Chapter One

Not Friends Anymore

Although I resemble a creepy scarecrow, this photo brings back memories of a simpler time that involved hair scrunchies, jumping on the trampoline for hours, and my favorite Esprit T-shirt.

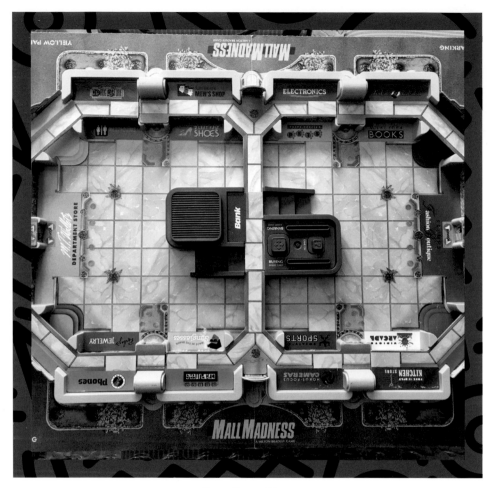

Best. Game. Ever.

When I think back to my childhood, I have many fond memories of being in elementary school. Although cliques were already starting to form, I had plenty of friends, and it seemed as though I was sleeping over at someone's house nearly every weekend. Those sleepovers were the best. We held talent shows, prank-called boys, and played games like Girl Talk and Mall Madness. I got along well with everyone; however, that all changed when I entered junior high.

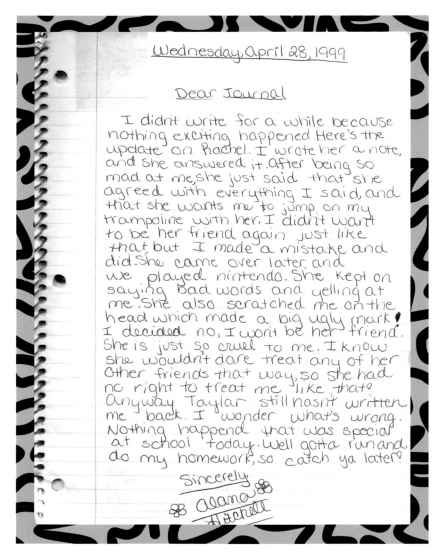

Wednesday, April 28, 1999

Dear Journal,

I didn't write for a while because nothing exciting happened Here's the update on Rachel. I wrote her a note, and she answered it. After being so mad at me, she just said that she agreed with everything I said, and that she wants me to jump on my trampoline with her. I didn't want to be her friend again just like that, but I made a mistake and did. She came over later, and we played nintendo. She kept on saying bad words and yelling at me. She also scratched me on the head which made a big ugly mark! I decided no, I won't be her friend. She is just so cruel to me. I know she wouldn't dare treat any of her other friends that way, so she had no right to treat me like that. Anyway Taylar still hasn't written me back. I wonder what's wrong. Nothing happend that was special at school today. Well gotta run and do my homework, so catch ya later!

Sincerely
Alana Nichell

(Age 13)

How dare Rachel accidentally scratch me on the head. I'm not sure why my pen pal, Taylar, never wrote me back, but I'm guessing it had something to do with how crazy and dramatic I was.

My neighbors trusted me to watch their dog, Blackie, while they were on vacation, and what did I do? I immediately lost him for about twelve hours during a thunderstorm. I had a legitimate reason for being so mad at Anna—she beat me at Mario Kart 64.

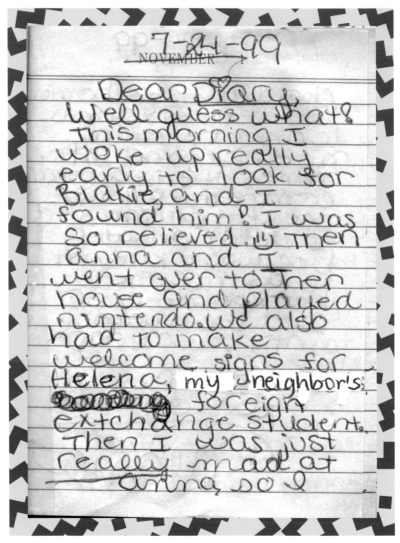

7-24-99
~~NOVEMBER~~ →

Dear Diary,
Well guess what?
This morning I
woke up really
early to look for
Blakie, and I
found him! I was
so relieved. Then
anna and I
went over to her
house and played
nintendo. We also
had to make
welcome signs for
Helena, my neighbor's
~~bowling~~ foreign
exchange student.
Then I was just
really mad at
anna, so I

(Age 14)

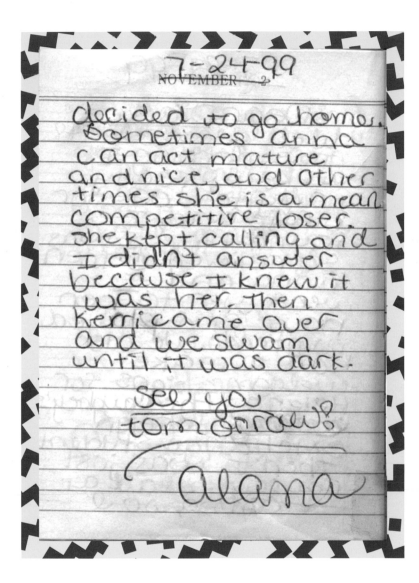

7-24-99
NOVEMBER 2

decided to go home.
Sometimes anna
can act mature
and nice, and Other
times she is a mean
competitive loser.
She kept calling and
I didn't answer
because I knew it
was her. Then
Kerri came over
and we swam
until it was dark.

see ya
tomorrow?

alana

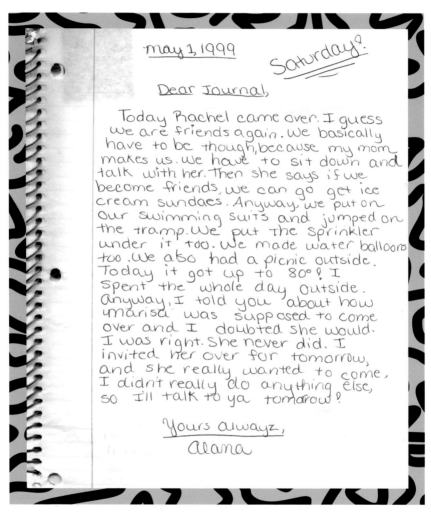

May 1, 1999   Saturday!

Dear Journal,

Today Rachel came over. I guess we are friends again. We basically have to be though, because my mom makes us. We have to sit down and talk with her. Then she says if we become friends, we can go get ice cream sundaes. Anyway, we put on our swimming suits and jumped on the tramp. We put the sprinkler under it too. We made water balloons too. We also had a picnic outside. Today it got up to 80°! I spent the whole day outside. Anyway, I told you about how umarisa was supposed to come over and I doubted she would. I was right. She never did. I invited her over for tomorrow, and she really wanted to come. I didn't really do anything else, so I'll talk to ya tomorrow!

Yours alwayz,
Alana

(Age 13)

The constant back and forth with my neighbor even stressed my mom out. It was time to step in with a plan—bribing us with ice cream sundaes.

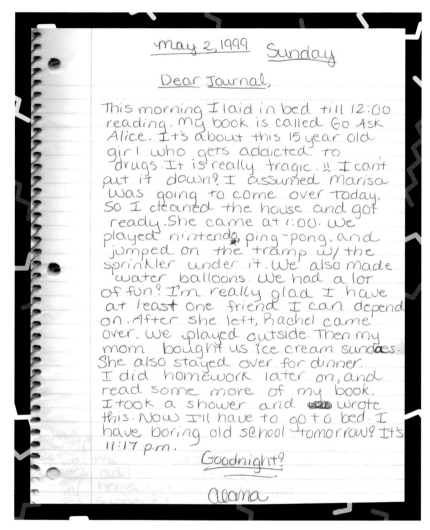

may 2, 1999   Sunday

Dear Journal,

This morning I laid in bed till 12:00 reading. My book is called Go Ask Alice. It's about this 15 year old girl who gets addicted to drugs. It is really tragic.!! I can't put it down? I assumed Marisa was going to come over today, so I cleaned the house and got ready. She came at 1:00. We played nintendo, ping-pong, and jumped on the tramp w/ the sprinkler under it. We also made water balloons. We had a lot of fun? I'm really glad I have at least one friend I can depend on. After she left, Rachel came over. We played outside. Then my mom bought us ice cream sundaes. She also stayed over for dinner. I did homework later on, and read some more of my book. I took a shower and wrote this. Now I'll have to go to bed. I have boring old school tomorrow? It's 11:17 p.m.

   Goodnight?

   alana

(Age 13)

The ice cream sundae plan seemed to work like a charm.

When my friend didn't come over to play one last round of The Game of Life before leaving for camp in New York, I decided maybe it'd be best if she just moved there. I tried to act tough like I wouldn't miss her at all, but I'm pretty sure I started writing her a letter before she even arrived at camp.

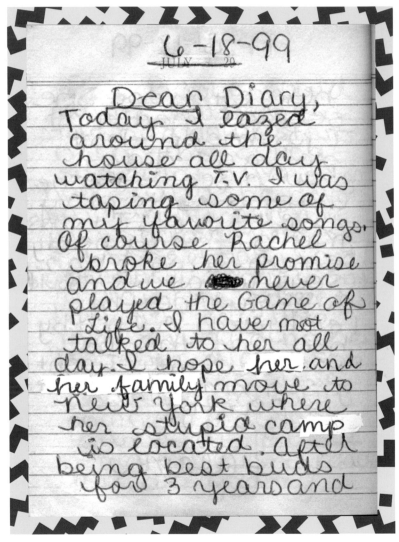

6-18-99
~~JULY 20~~

Dear Diary,
Today I lazed around the house all day watching T.V. I was taping some of my favorite songs. Of course Rachel broke her promise and we never played the Game of Life. I have not talked to her all day. I hope her and her family move to New York where her stupid camp is located. After being best buds for 3 years and

(Age 13)

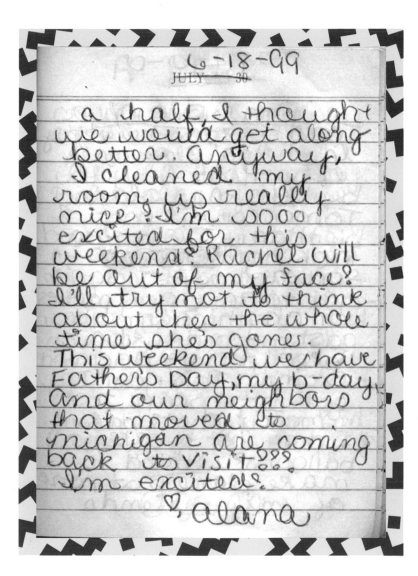

6-18-99
JULY 30

a half, I thought
we would get along
better. Anyway,
I cleaned my
room up really
nice! I'm soooo
excited for this
weekend! Rachel will
be out of my face!
I'll try not to think
about her the whole
time she's gone.
This weekend we have
Father's Day, my b-day,
and our neighbors
that moved to
michigan are coming
back to visit???
I'm excited!
♡ alana

It wasn't only my neighbor who I couldn't get along with. I invited my friend, Kerri, to sleep over and attend a talent show. When she didn't confirm the plan, I started to get suspicious about her going with our other friend, Marisa. I claimed that I only called Marisa to find out what time the talent show started, but clearly, I had other intentions. In the end, I decided the mature thing to do was show up at the talent show with my sister and completely ignore them.

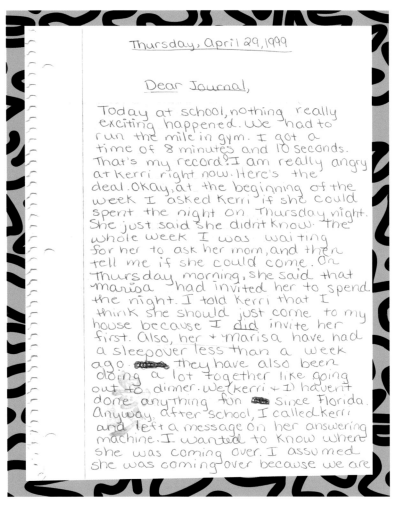

Thursday, April 29, 1999

Dear Journal,

Today at school, nothing really exciting happened. We had to run the mile in gym. I got a time of 8 minutes and 10 seconds. That's my record! I am really angry at Kerri right now. Here's the deal. Okay, at the beginning of the week I asked Kerri if she could spent the night on Thursday night. She just said she didn't know. The whole week I was waiting for her to ask her mom, and then tell me if she could come. On Thursday morning, she said that Marisa had invited her to spend the night. I told Kerri that I think she should just come to my house because I did invite her first. Also, her + Marisa have had a sleepover less than a week ago. they have also been doing a lot together like going out to dinner. We (kerri + I) haven't done anything fun since Florida. Anyway, after school, I called Kerri and left a message on her answering machine. I wanted to know when she was coming over. I assumed she was coming over because we are

(Age 13)

better friends anyway. I also wanted
to invite her to a talent show that
was playing at the high school. I
called Marisa to see what time
it was (the show) and she said
Kerri was over. I was sooo mad?
I still am? Kerri just went to her
house to sleep over without even
telling me? I invited her first?
I cried for a long time. I decided
I didnt want her to ruin my
night, so my sister & I went
to the talent show together.
Marisa and Kerri were there,
but I tried to ignore them.
I ended up having a good time.
There was a lot of singing. Nobody
won though. Well thats all for
today?

Sincerely,

Alana

This
means ——→
love

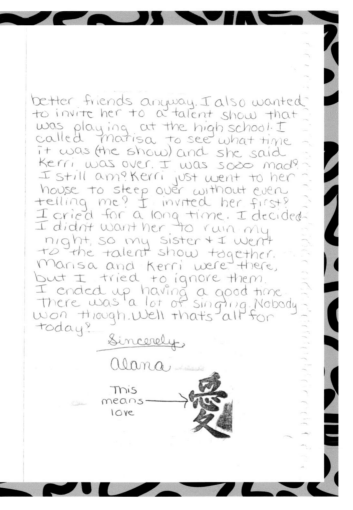

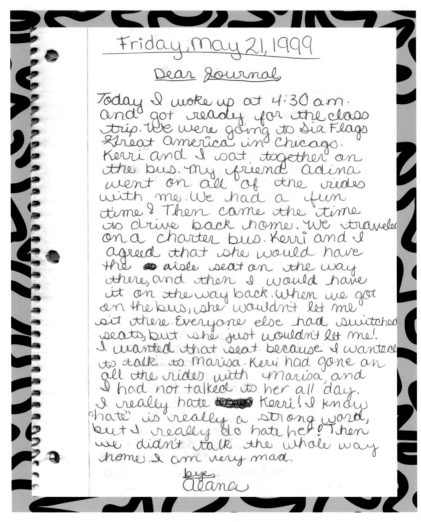

Friday, May 21, 1999

Dear Journal

Today I woke up at 4:30 a.m. and got ready for the class trip. We were going to Six Flags Great America in Chicago. Kerri and I sat together on the bus. My friend Adina went on all of the rides with me. We had a fun time! Then came the time to drive back home. We traveled on a charter bus. Kerri and I agreed that she would have the aisle seat on the way there, and then I would have it on the way back. When we got on the bus, she wouldn't let me sit there. Everyone else had switched seats, but she just wouldn't let me! I wanted that seat because I wanted to talk to Marisa. Kerri had gone on all the rides with Marisa, and I had not talked to her all day. I really hate Kerri! I know "hate" is really a strong word, but I really do hate her! Then we didn't talk the whole way home. I am very mad.

bye
Alana

(Age 13)

It's interesting that I said my friend and I had a fun time riding on all the rides, when that wasn't what happened at all. Maybe I didn't want my diary to know the truth—that I was too scared to ride anything that went upside down (which happened to be the majority of the rides). I don't think I'll ever forget how upset I was about not getting that darn aisle seat.

After four days of not speaking to Kerri due to the aisle incident, I decided I was ready to be friends again. I was relieved when she randomly showed up at my door and thought we'd finally have a chance to talk things out. That is, until I realized she was only there to deliver my cookie dough.

Tuesday, May 25, 1999

Dear Journal,

I am really happy because we have not had any home-work yesterday or today! People said we wouldn't the whole rest of the week! Finally I can relax after a hard day at school. Kerri and I got in a fight last Friday (the class trip) and still have not made up. Right when I called her to make up, the doorbell rang. Guess who it was! Kerri of course. I hoped she had wanted to talk, but she just had to drop off some cookie dough I bought from her for a fund raiser. It was for her cheerleading camp. I e-mailed her over the weekend and have gotten no answer. Every time at school when I look at Kerri she looks mad. What is she mad about I wonder? I didn't do anything to her to make her mad - she did something to me. Well thats about all for today. I am going to call Kerri now and try to make up. Bye!

Alana Hitchell

(Age 13)

Continued on next page

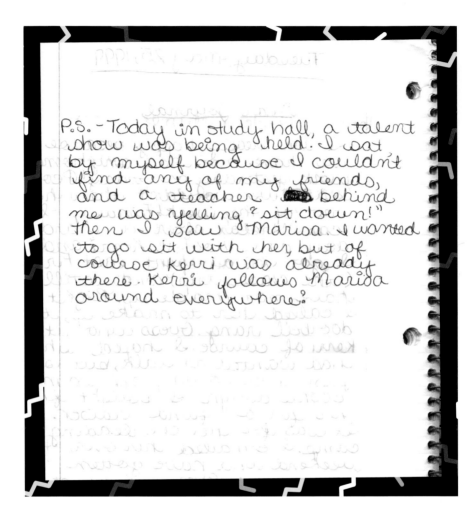

P.S. - Today in study hall, a talent show was being held. I sat by myself because I couldn't find any of my friends, and a teacher [illegible] behind me was yelling "sit down!" then I saw Marisa. I wanted to go sit with her, but of course Kerri was already there. Kerri follows Marisa around everywhere.

I have two questions regarding the postscript: could I truly not find any of my friends to sit with (or did I just not have any?) and how many talent shows did our school have?

One of the most memorable events of middle school was when my best friend and I took a trip to Florida. My friend wanted to make sure we had the best time possible and didn't forget any essentials, so she created a packing list. By the number of items on the list, you'd think we were leaving for two months instead of one week. You can tell it's the '90s by the items listed: Casio Pet Action, tapes, Game Boy/Game Gear games, scrunchies, and sparkling body splash. Not to mention the lovely clip art and reminder to tape *Frasier* for my older sister. What the heck is "gooey stuff," and why were we bringing homework on vacation? Luckily, I remembered to bring my diary—but forgot to pack my good mood.

Continued on next page

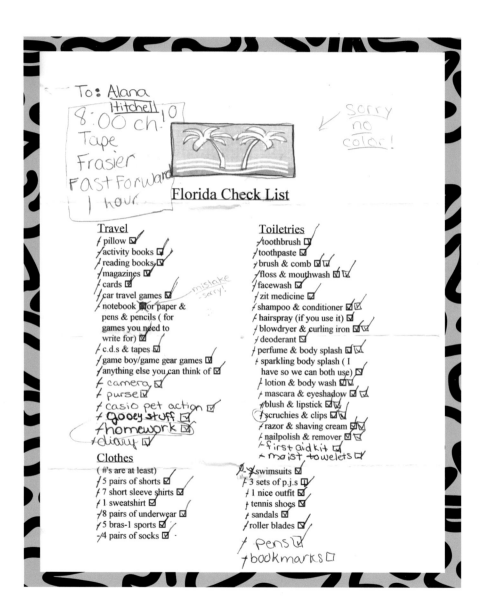

To: Alana Hitchell
8:00 ch. 10
Tape
Frasier
FastForward
1 hour

SORRY no color!

Florida Check List

Travel
- pillow ☑
- activity books ☑
- reading books ☑
- magazines ☑
- cards ☑
- car travel games ☑   mistake -sorry!
- notebook (or paper & pens & pencils (for games you need to write for) ☑
- c.d.s & tapes ☑
- game boy/game gear games ☑
- anything else you can think of ☑
- camera ☑
- purse ☑
- casio pet action ☑
- gooey stuff ☑
- homework ☑
- diary ☑

Clothes
(#'s are at least)
- 5 pairs of shorts ☑
- 7 short sleeve shirts ☑
- 1 sweatshirt ☑
- 8 pairs of underwear ☑
- 5 bras-1 sports ☑
- 4 pairs of socks ☑

Toiletries
- toothbrush ☑
- toothpaste ☑
- brush & comb ☑☑
- floss & mouthwash ☑☑
- facewash ☑
- zit medicine ☑
- shampoo & conditioner ☑☑
- hairspray (if you use it) ☑
- blowdryer & curling iron ☑☑
- deodorant ☑
- perfume & body splash ☑☑
- sparkling body splash (I have so we can both use) ☑
- lotion & body wash ☑☑
- mascara & eyeshadow ☑☑
- blush & lipstick ☑☑
- scruchies & clips ☑☑
- razor & shaving cream ☑☑
- nailpolish & remover ☑☑
- first aid kit ☑
- moist towelets ☑

- swimsuits ☑
- 3 sets of p.j.s ☑
- 1 nice outfit ☑
- tennis shoes ☑
- sandals ☑
- roller blades ☑

- pens ☑
- bookmarks ☐

Accessories
- earrings ☑
- necklaces ☑
- bracelets ☑
- anklets ☑
- rings ☑
- earplugs ☑
- eardrops ☑
- medicine ☑

Swimming/beach gear
- suntan lotion ☑
- goggles (Alana, if you can bring 2, because mine broke) ☑ ☑
- rafts ☑
- diving sticks ☑
- beach towel ☑
- beach bag ☑
- sunglasses ☑
- snorkel set ☑

P.S.- Be sure to pack another bag (other than your suitcase) to pack a swimsuit, change of 2 sets of clothes, p.j.s, and basic toiletries for the 2 night hotel stay.

P.P.S.- Don't forget to pack your security, excitement, and good mood!!

I'm finally done packing!

FLORIDA

If there's anything else you can think of add it to your list and tell me!

HAVE FUN PACKING!

We absolutely could not wait for our big trip to Florida. We talked endlessly about it for months and even had a countdown going in our assignment notebooks. Unfortunately, things didn't quite go as planned . . .

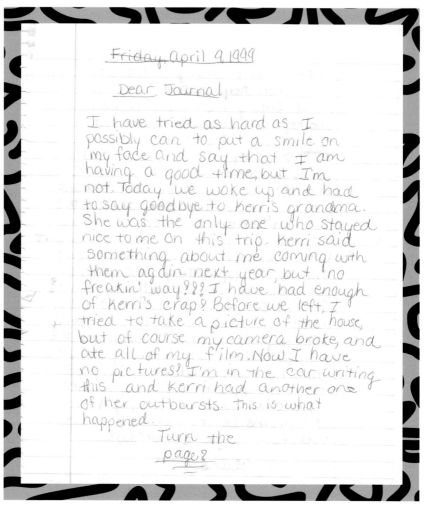

Friday, April 9, 1999

Dear Journal,

I have tried as hard as I possibly can to put a smile on my face and say that I am having a good time, but I'm not. Today we woke up and had to say goodbye to kerri's grandma. She was the only one who stayed nice to me on this trip. kerri said something about me coming with them again next year, but no freakin' way??? I have had enough of kerri's crap? Before we left, I tried to take a picture of the house, but of course my camera broke, and ate all of my film. Now I have no pictures? I'm in the car writing this and kerri had another one of her outbursts. This is what happened. Turn the page?

(Age 13)

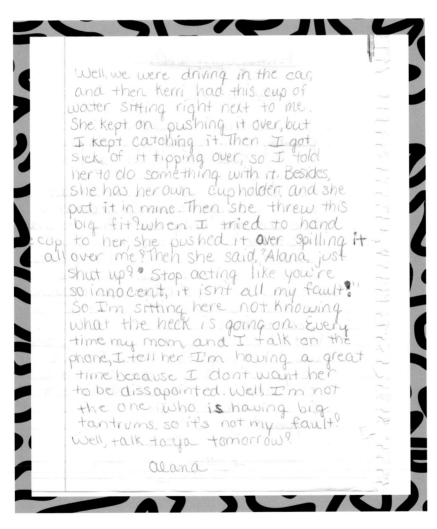

Well, we were driving in the car, and then Kerri had this cup of water sitting right next to me. She kept on pushing it over, but I kept catching it. Then I got sick of it tipping over, so I told her to do something with it. Besides, she has her own cup holder, and she put it in mine. Then she threw this big fit? when I tried to hand cup to her, she pushed it over spilling it all over me? Then she said, "Alana, just shut up? Stop acting like you're so innocent, it isn't all my fault?" So I'm sitting here not knowing what the heck is going on. Every time my mom and I talk on the phone, I tell her I'm having a great time because I don't want her to be dissapointed. Well I'm not the one who is having big tantrums, so it's not my fault? Well, talk to ya tomorrow?

Alana

I made myself sound awfully innocent, but I'm guessing there was more to that water cup story.

none			
H	O	O	L

Parent Sig.

Teacher Comments:

The word "teamwork" is often used in association with athletics. However, teamwork relates to nearly every group situation. True teamwork requires effort by every member to achieve the goals the group has set for itself. Each member assumes a different role and does the best they can to perform his or her tasks. Teamwork leads to success – together, everyone achieves more.

The end of the countdown in my assignment notebook.

Only in Florida will you find manatee mailboxes.

Sunglasses would have been helpful.

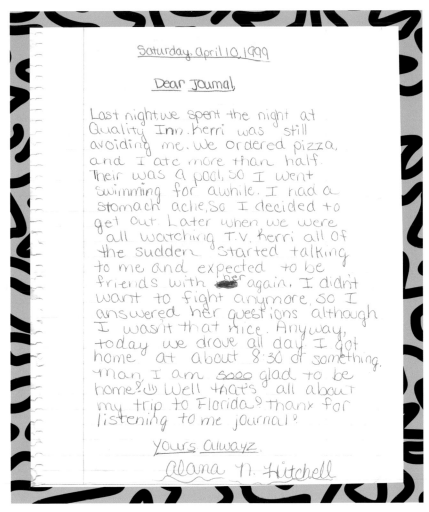

Saturday, April 10, 1999

Dear Journal,

Last night we spent the night at Quality Inn. Kerri was still avoiding me. We ordered pizza, and I ate more than half. Their was a pool, so I went swimming for awhile. I had a stomach ache, so I decided to get out. Later when we were all watching T.V. Kerri all of the sudden started talking to me and expected to be friends with ~~her~~ again. I didn't want to fight anymore, so I answered her questions although I wasn't that nice. Anyway, today we drove all day. I got home at about 8:30 of something. Man, I am soooo glad to be home! :) Well that's all about my trip to Florida! Thanx for listening to me journal!

Yours Alwayz,

Alana M. Hitchell

(Age 13)

Eating more than half a pizza before going swimming is never a good idea.

Chapter Two

Discovering Boys

This was my "model" pose, although I bear more resemblance to a deer caught in the headlights.

I can still remember my first crush. I was in fourth grade and had the hots for a guy in my class named Justin. Once the teacher announced we could bring in anything for show-and-tell, I immediately knew what I wanted to bring: my two guinea pigs. I felt like this was my big chance to impress Justin. My brother, who was a year ahead of me in school, also wanted to bring the guinea pigs, so my parents explained that my brother would show them to his class first and then I could show them to mine the next day. Of course, that wasn't good enough for me—I needed to get Justin to like me ASAP! I couldn't wait one extra day and argued with my parents until they agreed to let me bring the guinea pigs in first. I was beyond excited on the day of show-and-tell until I found out that Justin was sick and didn't come to school. Although distraught, I certainly learned a lesson early on about being patient.

Rest in peace, Nibbles and Squeaker. A few things come to mind when I think about them: the time my mom thought it looked like someone had given them a haircut and was convinced it was me, their untimely death because our pet sitter had forgotten to give them water while we were on vacation, and the time I was curious about death and attempted to dig them up in the backyard.

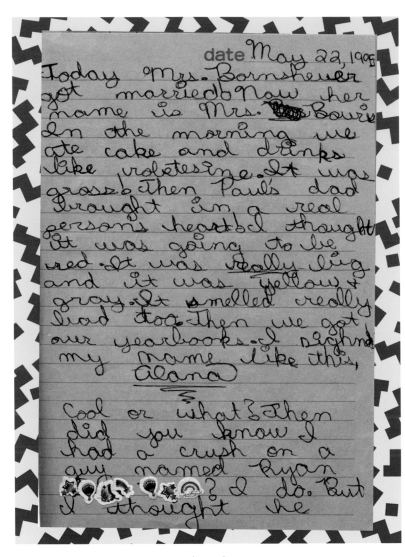

date May 22, 1905

Today Mrs. Bornsheuer got married. Now her name is Mrs. ~~Boo~~ Bouri. In the morning we ate cake and drinks like robitesine. It was grass. Then Paul's dad brought in a real persons heart. I thought it was going to be red. It was really big and it was yellow + gray. It smelled really bad too. Then we got our yearbooks. I sighnd my name like this,

__Alana__

Cool or what? Then did you know I had a crush on a guy named Ryan ? I do. But I thought he

(Age 9)

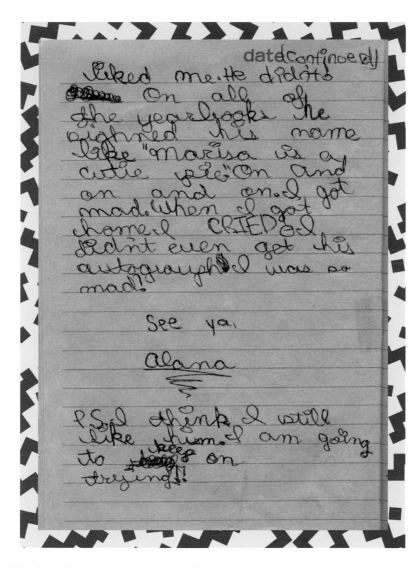

date(continued)

liked me. He did it
On all of
the yearbooks. He
signed his name
like "Marisa is a
cutie pie." On and
on and on. I got
mad. When I got
home, I CRIED. I
didn't even get his
autograph! I was so
mad!

See ya,

Alana

P.S. I think I still
like him. I am going
to keep on
trying!!

I probably should have mentioned that Paul's dad was a doctor and brought the heart in during science class. I was devastated when I noticed that instead of simply signing his name in people's yearbooks, Ryan added a little something extra: *Marisa is a cutie pie*.

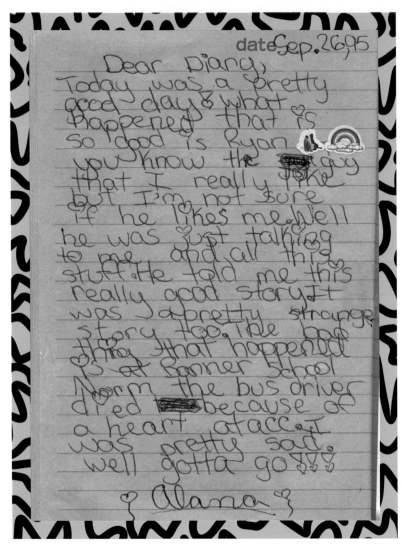

date Sep. 26, 95

Dear Diary,
Today was a pretty
good day & what is
happened that is
so good is Ryan
you know the guy
that I really like
but I'm not sure
if he likes me. Well
he was just talking
to me and all this
stuff. He told me this
really good story. It
was a pretty strange
story too. The bad
thing that happened
is at Bonner school
Norm the bus driver
died because of
a heart atacc. I
was pretty sad.
well gotta go

♡ Alana ♡

(Age 10)

I seemed to have gotten over the yearbook debacle pretty quickly. You know you're smitten when you dot your i's and exclamation points with hearts. Somehow, I didn't seem too upset about the bus driver passing away.

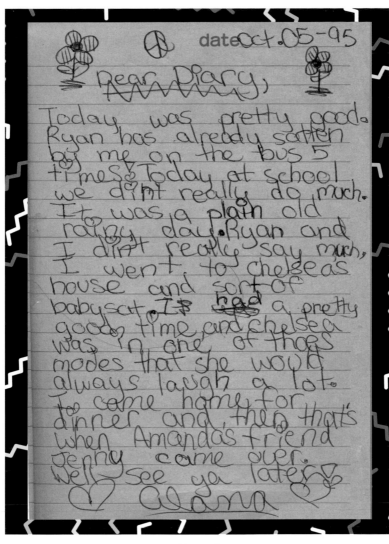

(Age 10)

I even kept track of how many times Ryan had "satten" by me on the bus.

By the time 1998 rolled around, I had moved on from Ryan to Nathan. I was sure he liked me, too, even though I don't recall any evidence of this. Note to self: don't talk badly about your neighbor in your diary and then leave it out in the open for her to find and make corrections.

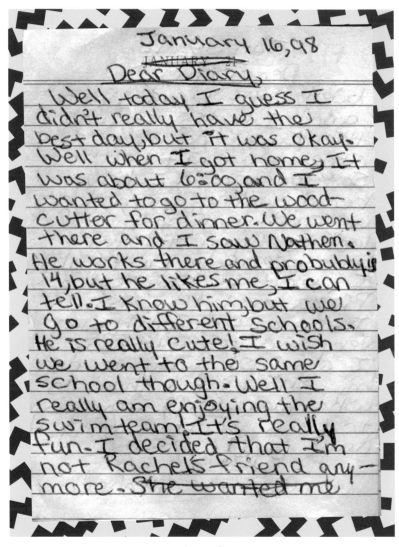

January 16, 98

~~JANUARY 21~~

Dear Diary,

Well today I guess I didn't really have the best day, but it was okay. Well when I got home, It was about 6:00, and I wanted to go to the wood-cutter for dinner. We went there and I saw Nathen. He works there and probuly is 14, but he likes me, I can tell. I know him, but we go to different schools. He is really cute! I wish we went to the same school though. Well I really am enjoying the swim-team! It's really fun. I decided that I'm not Rachel's friend any-more. She ~~wanted me~~

(Age 12)

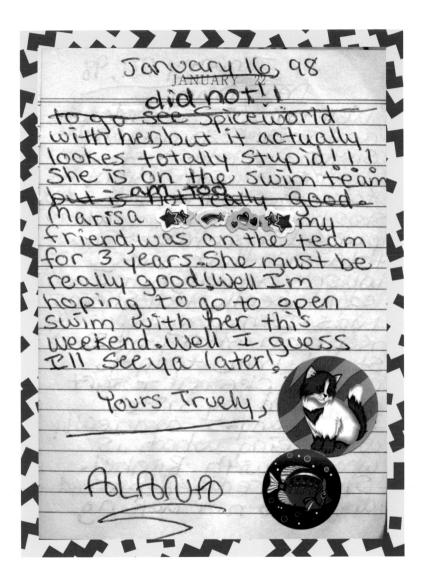

January 16, 98

~~JANUARY 22~~

did not!!

~~to go see~~ Spiceworld
with her, but it actually
lookes totally stupid!!!
She is on the swim team
~~but is not too really good.~~ am
Marisa my
friend, was on the team
for 3 years. She must be
really good! well I'm
hoping to go to open
swim with her this
weekend. well I guess
I'll see ya later!

Yours Truely,

ALANA

I loved Nathan, yet didn't know how to spell his name correctly.

Apparently, I told some of my classmates that Nathan was my boyfriend even though we had barely talked.

GO BLACK!

Dear Alana,

I really hope your team wins! You guys have really great coaches! I Guess your pretty happy your Boyfriend Nathen lives by you! I wish Lindsey would get hear. I hope her mom doesn't say anything to me! Blue looks sortof good. I think you may tie! Well goda go!

Love ya,
Laura

A few times throughout the summer, my parents drove us over to the high school for open swim. The deep end was a whopping twelve feet! I loved the challenge of jumping off the diving board, touching the bottom with my tippy toe, and then rapidly swimming back to the surface before running out of air. Sometimes it felt as though I had just barely made it. On this particular two-day trip to the pool, I learned the hard way that adolescent boys like to play games.

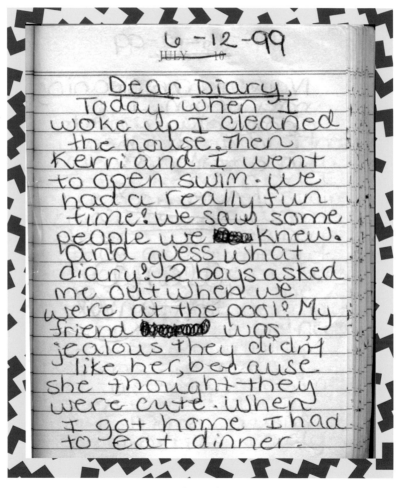

(Age 13)

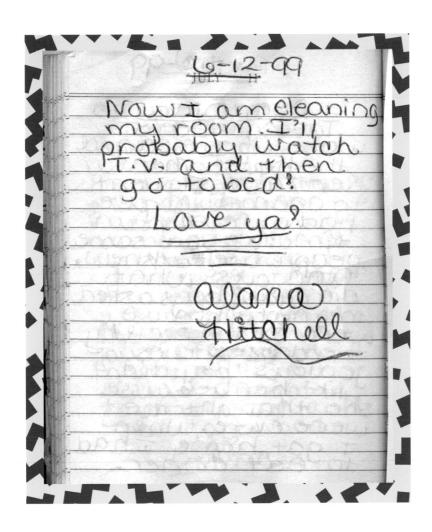

6-12-99
~~JULY 11~~

Now I am cleaning my room. I'll probably watch T.V. and then go to bed!

Love ya!

Alana Mitchell

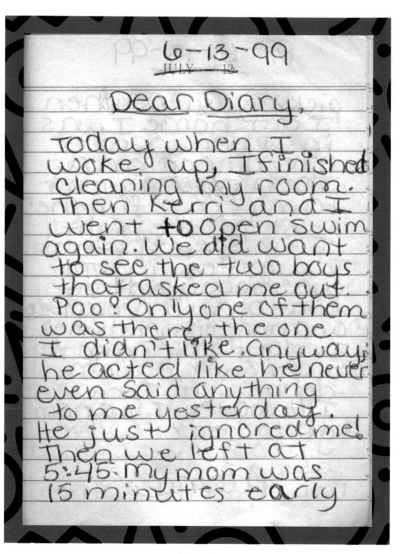

6-13-99
JULY — 12

Dear Diary,

Today when I
woke up, I finished
cleaning my room.
Then Kerri and I
went to open swim
again. We did want
to see the two boys
that asked me out.
Poo! Only one of them
was there, the one
I didn't like. Anyway,
he acted like he never
even said anything
to me yesterday.
He just ignored me!
Then we left at
5:45. My mom was
15 minutes early

(Age 13)

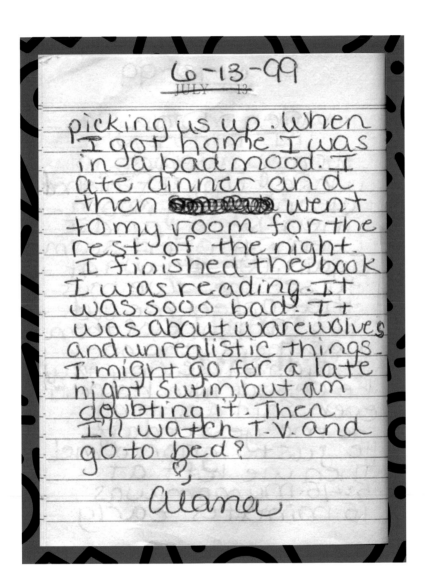

6-13-99
JULY 13

picking us up. When
I got home I was
in a bad mood. I
ate dinner and
then ~~scribbled out~~ went
to my room for the
rest of the night.
I finished the book
I was reading. It
was sooo bad. It
was about warewolves
and unrealistic things.
I might go for a late
night swim, but am
doubting it. Then
I'll watch T.V. and
go to bed?
♡,
Alana

After having several crushes on boys in my grade, I suddenly decided they were all immature freaks. I'm not sure what I so desperately needed money for, since I couldn't drive yet and my parents paid for everything.

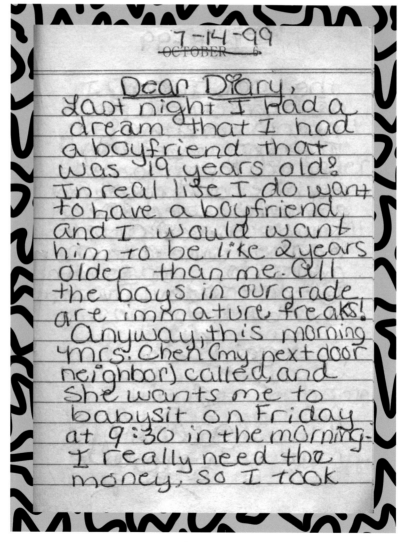

7-14-99
~~OCTOBER~~ 6

Dear Diary,
Last night I had a dream that I had a boyfriend that was 19 years old? In real life I do want to have a boyfriend, and I would want him to be like 2 years older than me. All the boys in our grade are immature freaks! Anyway, this morning Mrs. Chen (my next door neighbor) called, and she wants me to babysit on Friday at 9:30 in the morning. I really need the money, so I took

(Age 14)

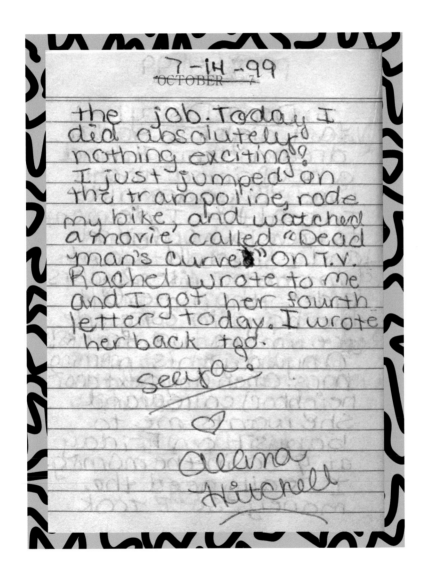

7-14-99
OCTOBER 7

the job. Today, I
did absolutely
nothing exciting?
I just jumped on
the trampoline, rode
my bike, and watched
a movie called "Dead
man's Curve" on T.V.
Rachel wrote to me
and I got her fourth
letter today. I wrote
her back too.
      seeya!
        ♡
      Alana
      Mitchell

After giving up on the freaks in my grade, my new plan was to go after my older brother's friends.

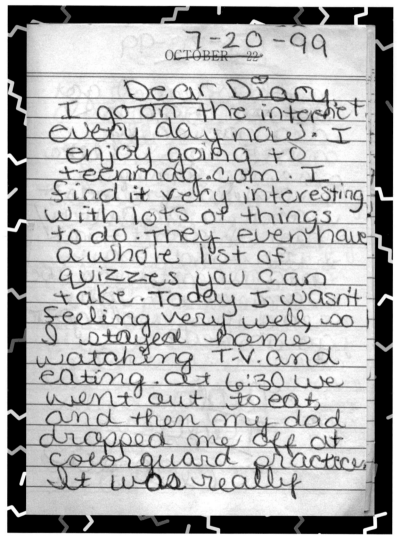

7-20-99
OCTOBER 22

Dear Diary,
I go on the internet
every day now. I
enjoy going to
teenmag.com. I
find it very interesting
with lots of things
to do. They even have
a whole list of
quizzes you can
take. Today I wasn't
feeling very well, so
I stayed home
watching T.V. and
eating. At 6:30 we
went out to eat,
and then my dad
dropped me off at
colorguard practice.
It was really

(Age 14)

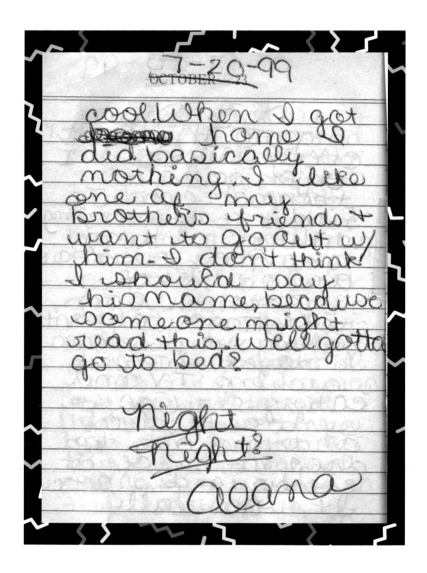

7-20-99
~~OCTOBER 23~~

cool. When I got
~~home~~ home
did basically
nothing. I like
one of my
brother's friends +
want to go out w/
him. I don't think
I should say
his name, because
some one might
read this. Well gotta
go to bed?

night
night?

Aana

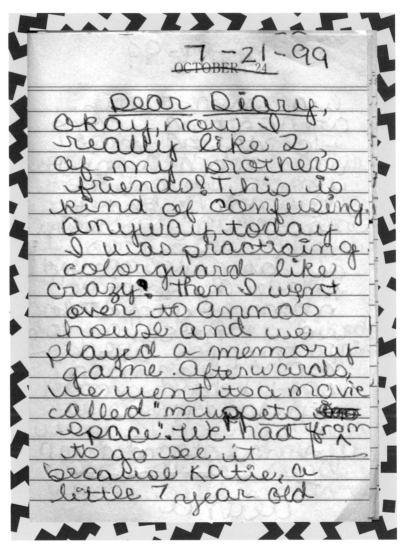

7 - 21 - 99
OCTOBER 24

Dear Diary,
Okay, now I really like 2 of my brother's friends! This is kind of confusing. Anyway, today I was practising colorguard like crazy! Then I went over to Anna's house and we played a memory game. Afterwards, we went to a movie called "muppets from space". We had to go see it because katie, a little 7 year old

(Age 14)

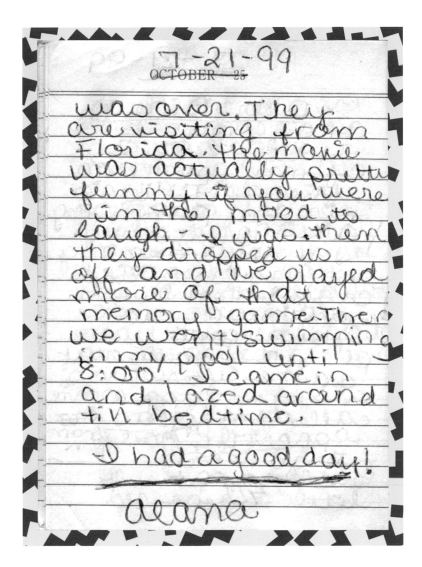

7-21-99

OCTOBER 25

was over. They
are visiting from
Florida. The movie
was actually pretty
funny if you were
in the mood to
laugh - I was. then
they dropped us
off and we played
more of that
memory game. Then
we went swimming
in my pool until
8:00. I came in
and lazed around
till bedtime.

I had a good day!

alana

If I was still going to see movies like *Muppets from Space*, I probably wasn't ready for dating.

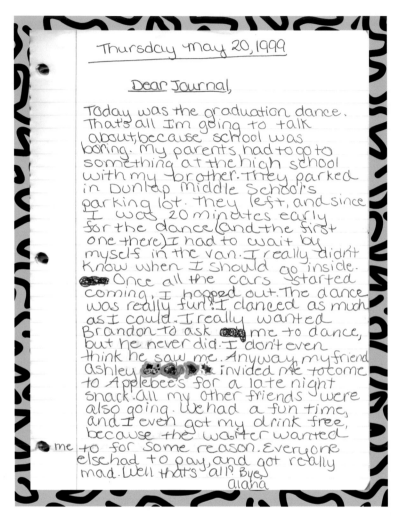

Thursday May 20, 1999

Dear Journal,

Today was the graduation dance. That's all I'm going to talk about, because school was boring. My parents had to go to something at the high school with my brother. They parked in Dunlap Middle School's parking lot. they left, and since I was 20 minutes early for the dance (and the first one there) I had to wait by myself in the van. I really didn't know when I should go inside. Once all the cars started coming, I hopped out. The dance was really fun! I danced as much as I could. I really wanted Brandon to ask me to dance, but he never did. I don't even think he saw me. Anyway, my friend Ashley invided me to come to Applebee's for a late night snack. All my other friends were also going. We had a fun time, and I even got my drink free, because the waiter wanted me to for some reason. Everyone else had to pay, and got really mad. Well that's all! Bye! aloha

(Age 13)

I was much too shy to flirt with or even talk to boys I had a crush on. I'm sure they didn't have the slightest clue I was pining for them since I never made any moves. I'd hope my crush would somehow receive the telepathic messages I was trying to send, which never seemed to work.

Sporting my new butterfly hair clips for eighth grade graduation.

I barely mentioned this Brandon guy in my diary until now, but suddenly decided I was in love with him. I have so many questions: why was I so upset to be graduating from eighth grade? Why did I burst into deep sobs just because an overplayed song was on the radio? Why did I feel like this day changed me in some significant way, and why did I write this entry as if it were a romantic novel?

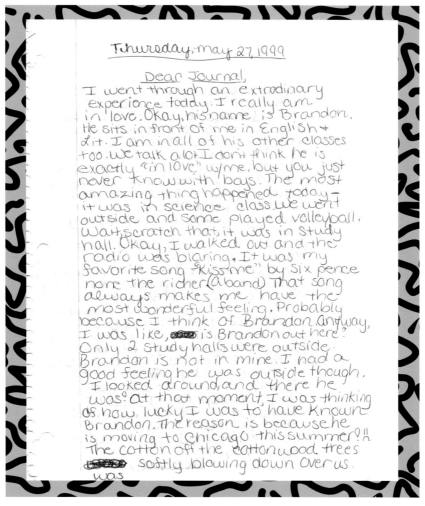

Thursday, May 27, 1999

Dear Journal,

I went through an extradinary experience today. I really am in love. Okay, his name is Brandon. He sits in front of me in English & Lit. I am in all of his other classes too. We talk a lot. I don't think he is exactly "in love" w/me, but you just never know with boys. The most amazing thing happened today — it was in science class we went outside and some played volleyball. Wait, scratch that it was in study hall. Okay, I walked out and the radio was blaring. It was my favorite song "kiss me" by six pence none the richer (a band) That song always makes me have the most wonderful feeling. Probably because I think of Brandon. Anyway, I was like, ⬛⬛⬛ is Brandon out here? Only 2 study halls were outside. Brandon is not in mine. I had a good feeling he was outside though. I looked around, and there he was! At that moment, I was thinking of how lucky I was to have known Brandon. The reason is because he is moving to Chicago this summer!! The cotton off the cottonwood trees ⬛⬛⬛ softly blowing down over us. was

(Age 13)

My song was still playing. Then it kind of turned into our song. I know every time I hear it after this day, it will always remind me of him. I was also thinking how much I would miss junior high. It makes me cry to think I'll never be going back. After I got home from school, I played outside a lot. I went on inside and up to my room. I was going to write in you, journal. I turned on the radio, and "Kiss me" was just starting!?!? At that moment, I burst into deep sobs. This day has changed me forever-in a way I could never explain. Tomorrow I graduate. I hope I don't start crying. Gosh, I'm supposed to be happy to be out of school. Marisa is really sad to leave too. Well this is the end of my journal. It is a good place to stop too. I _will_ be keeping another journal though. Thanks for listening to my life and its many problems.

-alana

Chapter Three

My Unhealthy Diet and Weather Woes

Wearing my hemp necklace and Yoyo jean shorts. You think you
have a good photo goin' on until the film is developed and you
realize that not only did the flash ruin it, but your sweater vest
didn't quite cover the top of your underwear.

PART ONE
MY UNHEALTHY DIET

The biggest theme I noticed while looking through my old diary entries (besides being dramatic) was food. Nearly half of my diary entries involved chronicling what I ate. Since both of my parents worked full time, there wasn't much time for cooking meals. I don't blame them at all because I currently don't have the time or energy to cook even *without* having kids, so my diet in the nineties primarily consisted of fast food, sweets, and frozen dinners. It's amazing I stayed so thin considering all of the horrible things I ate. Here are a few examples:

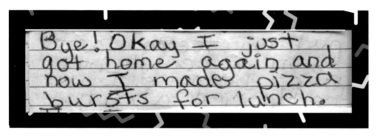

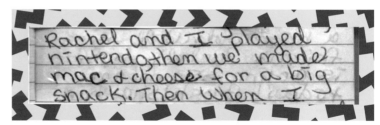

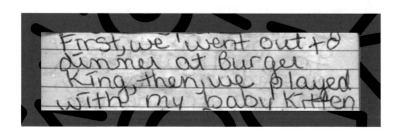

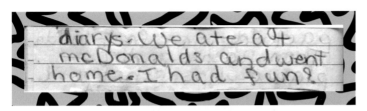

diarys. We ate at
mcDonalds and went
home. I had fun!

I ate 2 ice cream
cones, watched
Judge Judy, and
then went to bed.

When it was about
5:00, my mom, dad and
I went out to eat at
The woodcutter. I had
my favorite thing -
potato nachos! I watch

nintendo. We ate
some cheese dogs
because we were
still hungry. We then

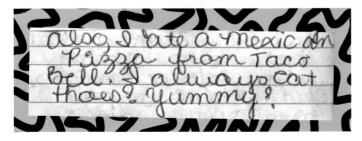

also, I ate a mexican
Pizza from Taco
Bell! I always eat
thoes! yummy!

6-27-99
AUGUST 19

We ate frozen
dinners. The rest of
the night I spent
watching TV.
although I did

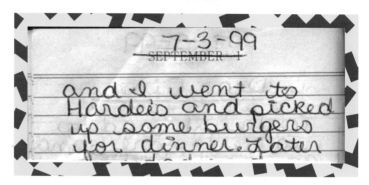

7-3-99
SEPTEMBER 1

and I went to
Hardees and picked
up some burgers
for dinner. Later

Then my mom and
I went to Dairy Queen
and got chili dogs.

7-15-99
OCTOBER 1

Then I went home
and went out to
eat w/my parents
at Arby's. I had a
chicken deluxe sand-
which. Then I got home

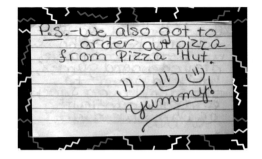

P.s.—We also got to order out pizza from Pizza 'Hut.
☺ ☺ ☺ yummy!

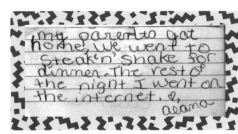

my parents got home, We went to Steak 'n' Shake for dinner. The rest of the night I went on the internet. ♥,
aeana

bad. Then we ate frappaccino ice cream bars! I went home after that.

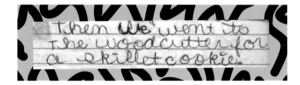

Then We went to the woodcutter for a skillet cookie.

school. We ate hot dogs and had a good time. We also

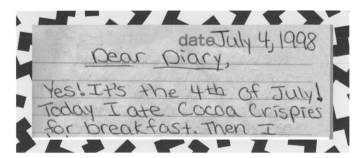

date July 4, 1998

Dear Diary,

Yes! It's the 4th of July! Today I ate Cocoa Crispies for breakfast. Then I

Several weeks before starting high school, I decided to join color guard. This required going to band camp to learn routines, how to march in parades, and how to do formations for field shows. Instead of writing about any of that in my diary, I chose to focus on something more important—what we had for lunch.

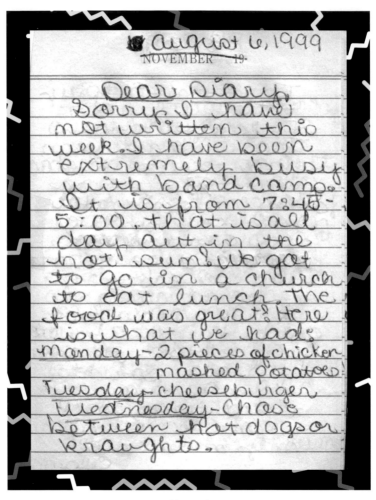

(Age 14.)

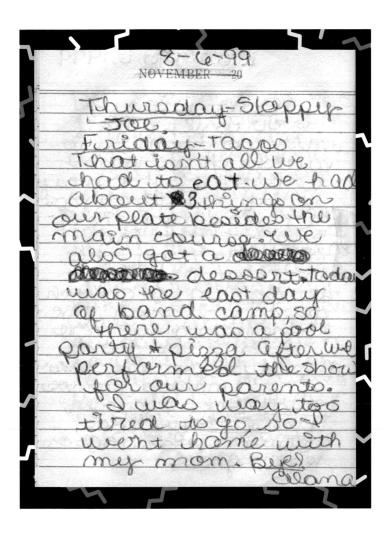

8-6-99

NOVEMBER — 20

Thursday-Sloppy
Joe,
Friday-tacos
That isn't all we
had to eat. We had
about 3 things on
our plate besides the
main course. we
also got a ~~dessert~~
~~dessert~~ dessert. today
was the last day
of band camp, so
there was a pool
party + pizza after we
performed the show
for our parents.
I was way too
tired to go, so I
went home with
my mom. Bye!
Alana

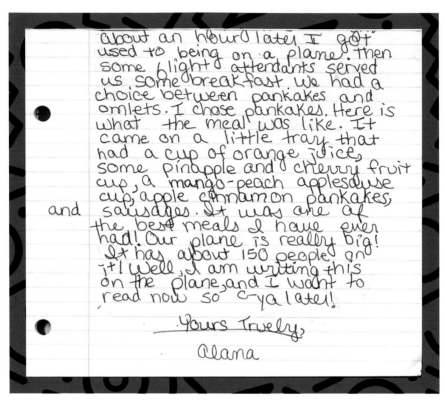

about an hour later, I got used to being on a plane. Then some flight attendants served us some breakfast. We had a choice between pankakes and omlets. I chose pankakes. Here is what the meal was like. It came on a little tray that had a cup of orange juice, some pinapple and cherry fruit cup, a mango-peach applesause cup, apple cinnamon pankakes, and sausages. It was one of the best meals I have ever had! Our plane is really big! It has about 150 people on it! Well, I am writing this on the plane, and I want to read now so c-ya later!

Yours Truely,

Alana

(Age 13)

Claiming that the breakfast we had on the plane from Chicago to Mexico was one of the best meals I'd ever had really says a lot about the type of crap I was eating at the time.

PART TWO
WEATHER WOES

Another main theme I noticed throughout my diary entries was complaining about the weather. At times, it seemed to control my entire mood. A good day could instantly turn into a bad one just because of a few clouds or drops of rain. I simply could not deal with weather ruining my plans, which seemed to happen quite often. Most people would still be willing to go swimming even if the weather turned a bit cloudy, but not me. If it wasn't perfectly sunny, then forget it. Here are a few examples of when the weather ruined my entire day.

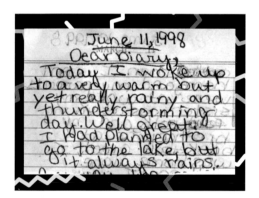

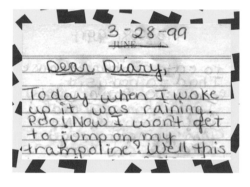

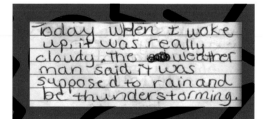

come over. At 3:30 I went swimming. Then there was storms coming, so I had to go inside.

June 2, 1999

Dear Diary,

Today my friend Kerri came over. We could not swim in the pool because it was really cloudy. Then Kerri's mom asked

6-10-99

Dear Diary,

Well today I was in my pajamas until 4:00. It was cloudy and raining, so I lazed around.

We had a fun time. The only bad thing was that it was really cold and cloudy outside.

Anyway my weekend has been awful. Rachel and I have been fighting constantly and it's cloudy. First

do??? My b-day has really been ruined by her and this 65° weather! Now I cant go swimming or have a party!

—Alana

Thursday May 6, 1999

Dear Journal,

Today it was really rainy and very cold! Its may, and I still have to wear jeans and a sweater. Anyway at school everything.

I was so outraged about the weather being unusually cold for June, that it required its own diary entry.

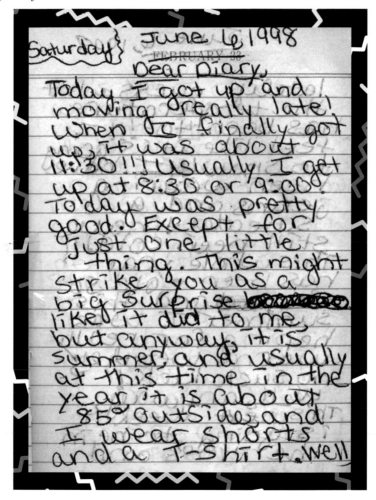

(Age 12)

Continued on next page

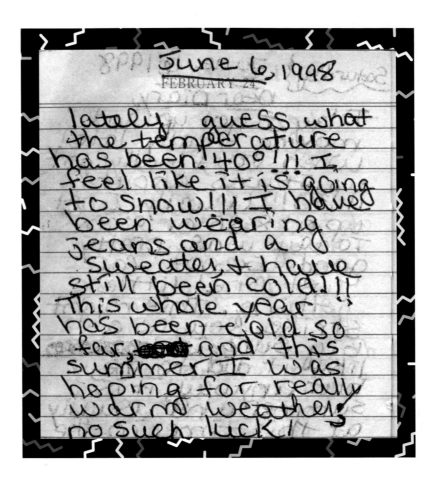

June 6, 1998

FEBRUARY 24

lately guess what
the temperature
has been. 40°!!! I
feel like it is going
to snow!!! I have
been wearing
jeans and a
sweater, + have
still been cold!!!
This whole year
has been cold so
far, and this
summer I was
hoping for really
warm weather.
no such luck!!

In my school journal, I was asked to write about what I would do in the event of a tornado warning. Apparently, it was more important to make sure that my money, irreplaceable material items, and cat made it down to the basement before my family did.

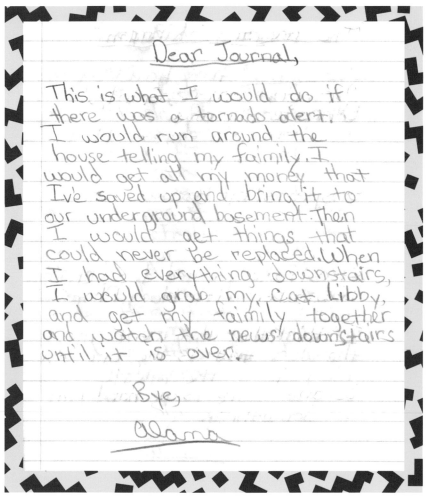

Dear Journal,

This is what I would do if there was a tornado alert. I would run around the house telling my faimily. I would get all my money that I've saved up and bring it to our underground basement. Then I would get things that could never be replaced. When I had everything downstairs, I would grab my Cat Libby, and get my faimily together and watch the news downstairs until it is over.

Bye,

Alana

(Age 11)

Chapter Four

Overly Dramatic

My brother and I went down to the lake behind our
house for an afternoon of fun that involved filling our
canoe with a bunch of frogs. My mom wasn't too thrilled
when we came home covered in mud.

As I'm sure you've noticed by now, I had a tendency to be quite dramatic. I was going through puberty at the time I wrote my most dramatic entries, but my behavior still seemed a bit over the top. I thought it was necessary to dedicate a chapter to my most embarrassing, yet hilarious diary entries of the times when I completely melted down.

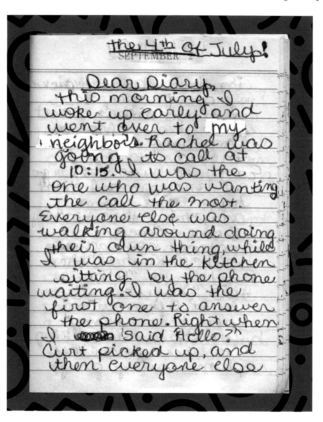

(Age 14)

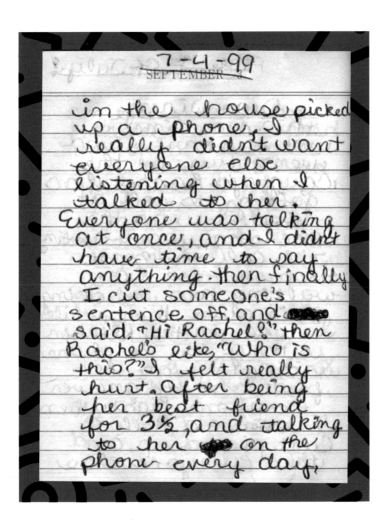

7-4-99
SEPTEMBER

in the house picked
up a phone, I
really didn't want
everyone else
listening when I
talked to her.
Everyone was talking
at once, and I didn't
have time to say
anything. then finally
I cut someone's
sentence off, and
said, "Hi Rachel!" then
Rachel's like, "Who is
this?" I felt really
hurt. After being
her best friend
for 3½, and talking
to her on the
phone every day,

Continued on next page

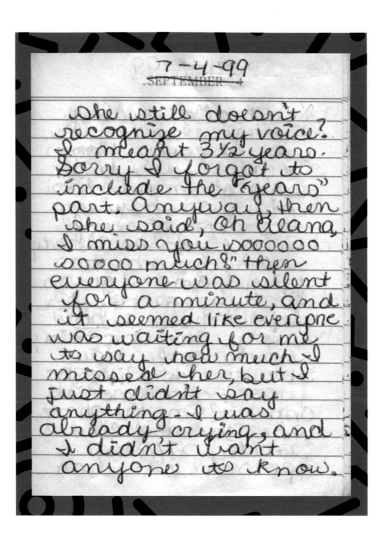

7-4-99
SEPTEMBER 4

She still doesn't
recognize my voice?
I meant 3½ years.
Sorry I forgot to
include the "years"
part. Anyway, then
she said, "Oh Reana,
I miss you sooooooo
ooooo much?" then
everyone was silent
for a minute, and
it seemed like everyone
was waiting for me
to say how much I
missed her, but I
just didn't say
anything. I was
already crying, and
I didn't want
anyone to know.

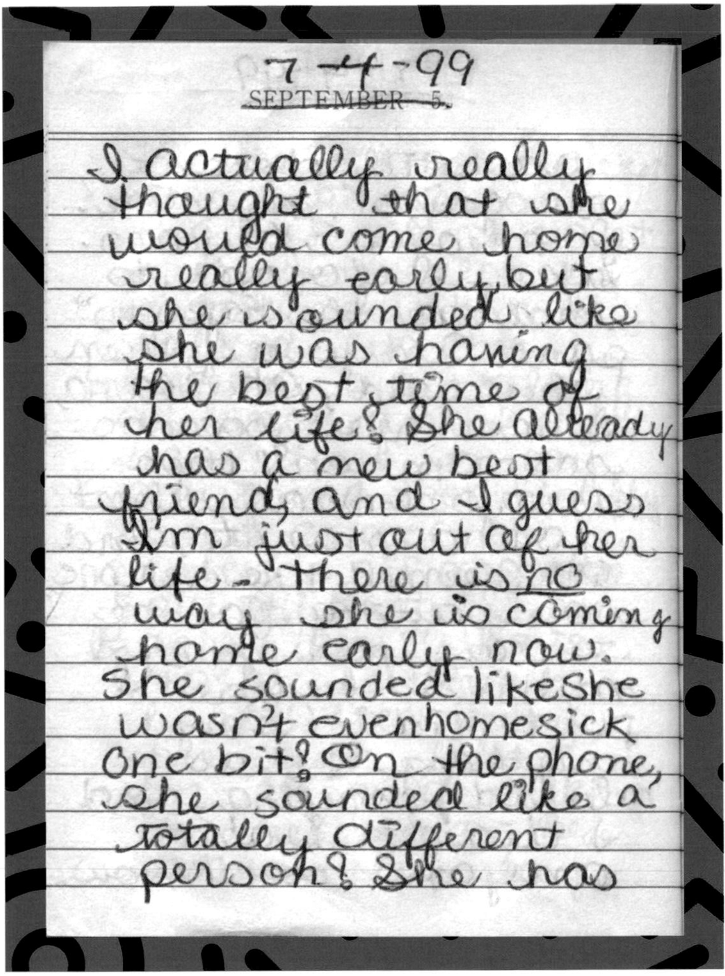

7-4-99

~~SEPTEMBER 5.~~

I actually really thought that she would come home really early, but she sounded like she was having the best time of her life? She already has a new best friend, and I guess I'm just out of her life - There is no way she is coming home early now. She sounded like she wasn't even homesick one bit? On the phone, she sounded like a totally different person? She has

Continued on next page

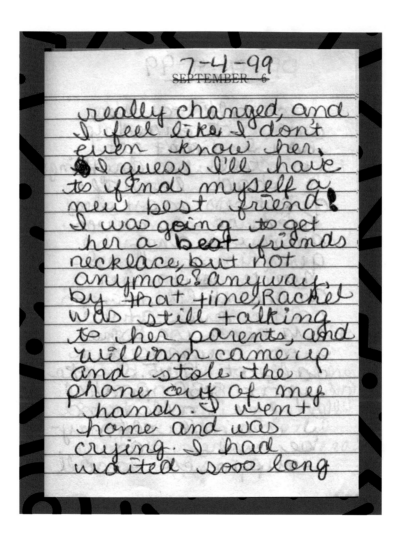

7-4-99
SEPTEMBER 6

really changed, and
I feel like I don't
even know her.
I guess I'll have
to find myself a
new best friend!
I was going to get
her a "best friends"
necklace, but not
anymore! anyway,
by that time, Rachel
was still talking
to her parents, and
william came up
and stole the
phone out of my
hands. I went
home and was
crying. I had
waited sooo long

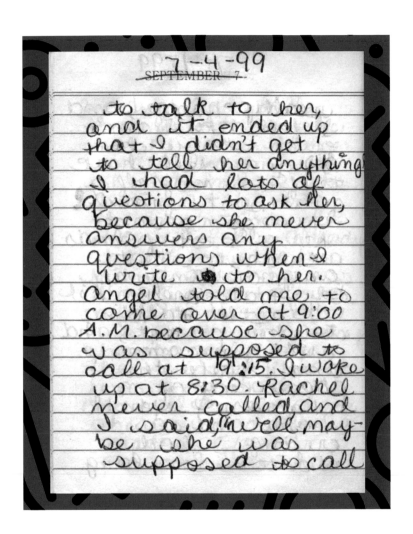

7-4-99
SEPTEMBER 7

to talk to her, and it ended up that I didn't get to tell her anything. I had lots of questions to ask her, because she never answers any questions when I write to her. Angel told me to come over at 9:00 A.M. because she was supposed to call at 9:15. I woke up at 8:30. Rachel never called and I said, "Well maybe she was supposed to call

Continued on next page

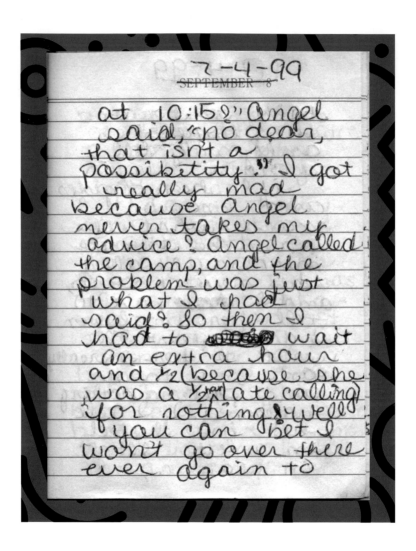

7-4-99
SEPTEMBER 8

at 10:15 ?" Angel
said, "no dear,
that isn't a
possibility." I got
really mad
because Angel
never takes my
advice ! Angel called
the camp, and the
problem was just
what I had
said ! So then I
had to ~~cancel~~ wait
an extra hour
and ½ (because she
was a ½ hr. late calling)
for nothing! well
you can bet I
won't go over there
ever again to

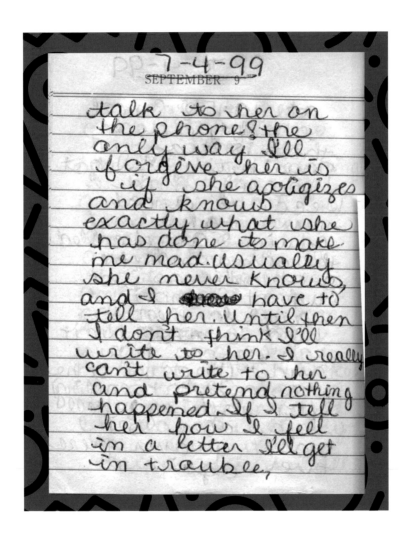

7-4-99

SEPTEMBER 9

talk to her on the phone? the only way I'll forgive her is if she apoligizes and knows exactly what she has done to make me mad. usually she never knows, and I ~~know~~ have to tell her. Until then I don't think I'll write to her. I really can't write to her and pretend nothing happened. If I tell her how I feel in a letter I'll get in trouble,

Continued on next page

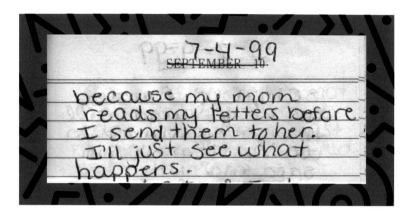

My neighbor had gone to camp in New York for the summer and didn't get to use the phone very often. It was a big deal when I heard she was going to call home, and I wanted to be there for it. Apparently, I was hoping she was miserable and wanted to come home early, but that wasn't the case. How dare she have fun and make new friends? Once I found out she was having a great time, giving her a friendship necklace was obviously out of the question.

When sleeping over at a friend's house, I anticipated that we would stay up all night playing games like Girl Talk, Dream Phone, and Truth or Dare. Simply watching a movie wasn't going to cut it. My disappointment turned into anger when I found out I had to sleep on the floor. Thank goodness that my diary was there to vent to.

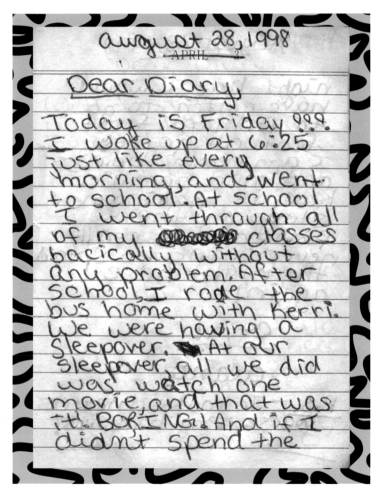

august 28, 1998
~~APRIL~~ 2

Dear Diary,

Today is Friday !!!. I woke up at 6:25 just like every morning, and went to school. At school I went through all of my ~~classes~~ classes bacically without any problem. After school, I rode the bus home with Kerri. We were having a sleepover. At our sleepover all we did was watch one movie, and that was it. BORING! And if I didn't spend the

(Age 13)

Continued on next page

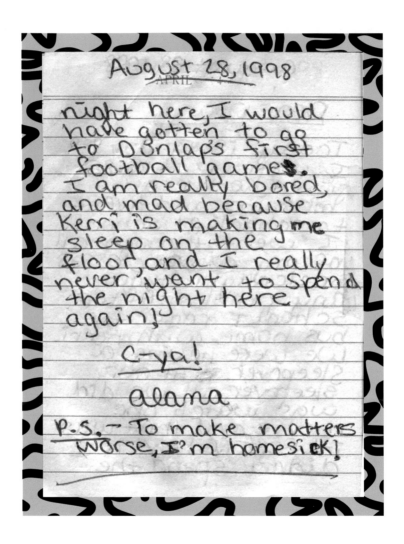

August 28, 1998
~~APRIL~~

night here, I would have gotten to go to Dunlap's first football games. I am really bored, and mad because Kerri is making me sleep on the floor, and I really never want to spend the night here again!

C-ya!

alana

P.S. - To make matters worse, I'm homesick!

I had extremely high expectations when it came to my birthday. Since my birthday is during the summer, I always wanted to have some sort of extravagant pool party with a cake, balloons, presents—the whole nine yards. (I think this might have even been the year I demanded a piñata.) If the weather didn't cooperate or some of my friends were on vacation, it sent me into a downward spiral.

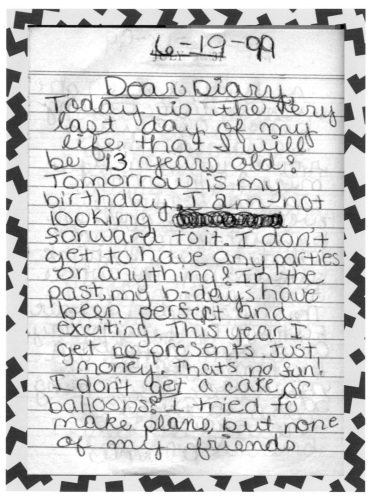

6-19-99
JULY 31

Dear Diary
Today is the very last day of my life that I will be 13 years old? Tomorrow is my birthday. I am not looking ~~forward~~ sorward to it. I don't get to have any parties or anything! In the past, my b-days have been persect and exciting. This year I get no presents. Just money. Thats no fun! I don't get a cake or balloons! I tried to make plans, but none of my friends

(Age 13)

Continued on next page

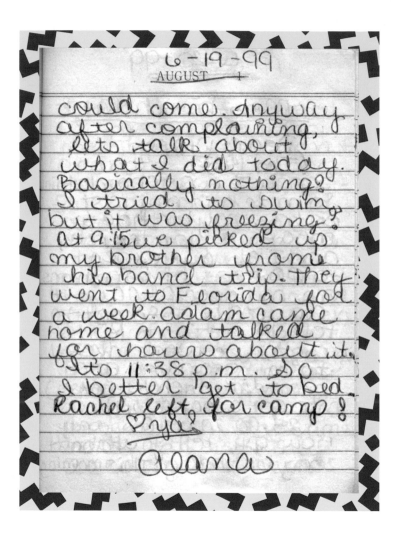

6-19-99
AUGUST

could come. Anyway
after complaining,
lets talk about
what I did today.
Basically nothing?
I tried to swim,
but it was freezing!
at 9:15 we picked up
my brother from
his band trip. they
went to Florida for
a week. adam came
home and talked
for hours about it.
Its 11:38 p.m. so
I better get to bed.
Rachel left for camp!
♥ya
Alana

My friend thought we could enjoy a nice afternoon playing with her new pet; however, I didn't seem to be the biggest fan of "hampsters," as I called them.

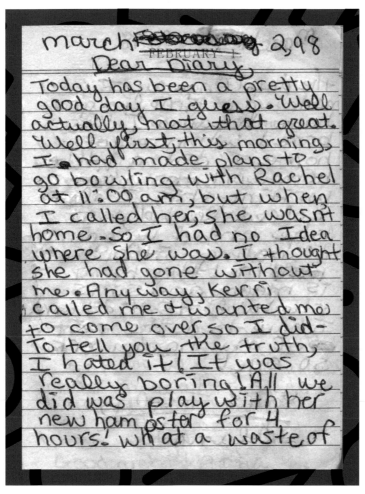

march ~~February~~ 2, 98
Dear Diary
Today has been a pretty good day I guess. Well actually, not that great. Well first, this morning, I had made plans to go bowling with Rachel at 11:00 am, but when I called her, she wasn't home. So I had no Idea where she was. I thought she had gone without me. Anyway, Kerri called me & wanted me to come over so I did - To tell you the truth, I hated it! It was really boring! All we did was play with her new hampster for 4 hours! what a waste of

(Age 12)

Continued on next page

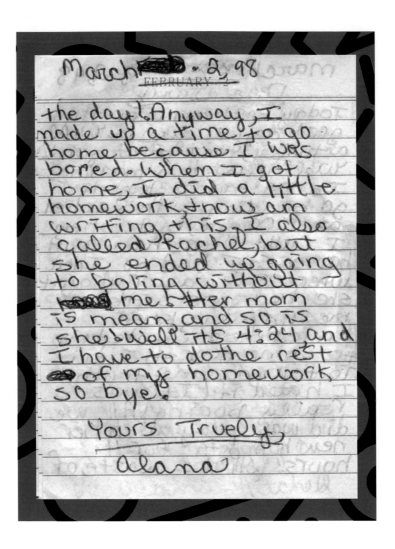

March ~~February 2~~ · 2, 98

the day!. Anyway, I made up a time to go home because I was bored. When I got home, I did a little homework + now am writing this. I also called Rachel, but she ended up going to boling without ~~me~~ me. Her mom is mean and so is she. Well it's 4:24 and I have to do the rest of my homework so bye!

Yours Truely

Alana

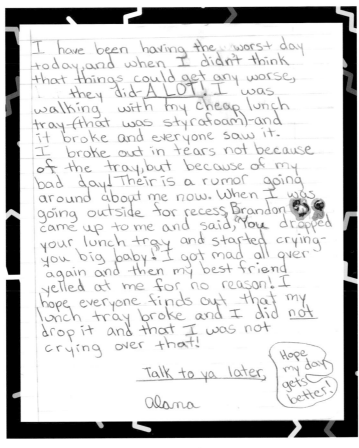

I have been having the worst day today, and when I didn't think that things could get any worse, they did A LOT! I was walking with my cheap lunch tray (that was styrofoam)-and it broke and everyone saw it. I broke out in tears not because of the tray, but because of my bad day! Their is a rumor going around about me now. When I was going outside for recess Brandon came up to me and said, "You dropped your lunch tray and started crying-you big baby! I got mad all over again and then my best friend yelled at me for no reason! I hope everyone finds out that my lunch tray broke and I did not drop it and that I was not crying over that!

Talk to ya later,

Alana

Hope my day gets better!

(Age 11)

When my Styrofoam lunch tray broke in sixth grade, it truly was the straw that broke the camel's back. I'm not sure why I was so adamant about wanting everyone to know that it broke as opposed to me dropping it. I'm guessing my super sensitivity was due to the fact that my family had teased me for years about my tendency to drop things. Ironically, the kid who called me a big baby is the same Brandon I claimed to be in love with in eighth grade.

Surprisingly, there were very few diary entries about me fighting with my siblings. When my parents went out on Saturday nights and left us home alone, we usually had a blast, but this night was a little different.

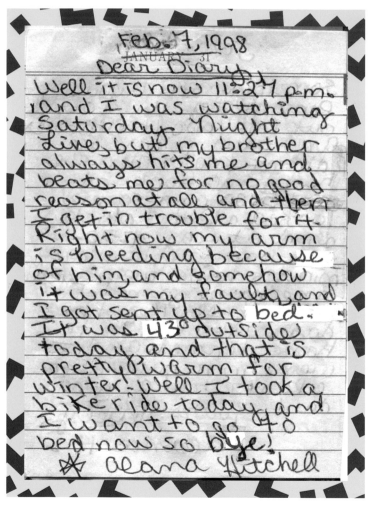

Feb. 7, 1998

~~JANUARY 31~~

Dear Diary,

Well it is now 11:27 p.m. and I was watching Saturday Night Live, but my brother always hits me and beats me for no good reason at all, and then I get in trouble for it. Right now my arm is bleeding because of him, and somehow it was my fault, and I got sent up to bed. It was 43° outside today, and that is pretty warm for winter. Well I took a bike ride today, and I want to go to bed now so bye!

☆ Alana Mitchell

(Age 12)

I even had kids at school worried about my safety.

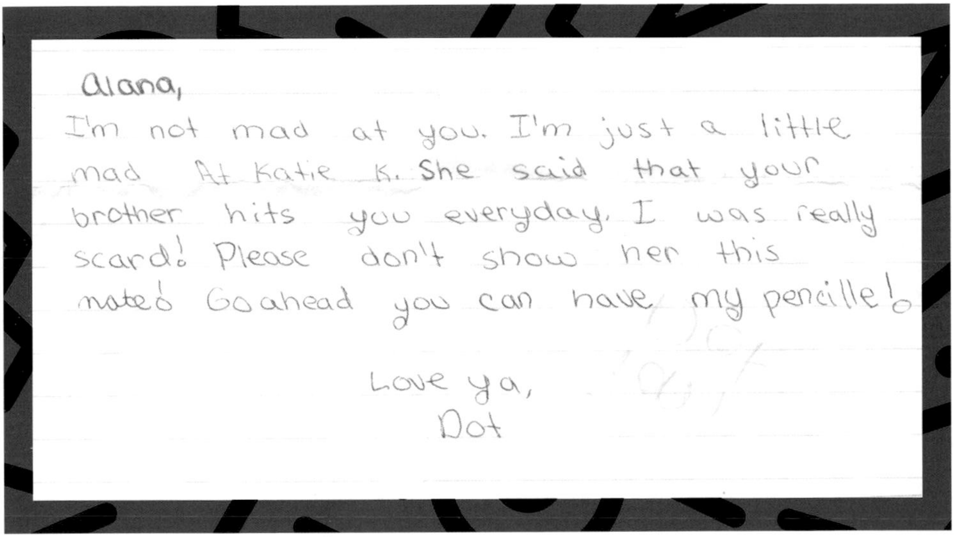

Alana,

I'm not mad at you. I'm just a little mad At Katie K. She said that your brother hits you everyday. I was really scard! Please don't show her this note. Go ahead you can have my pencille!

Love ya,
Dot

Not only was I beaten, I was also starved.

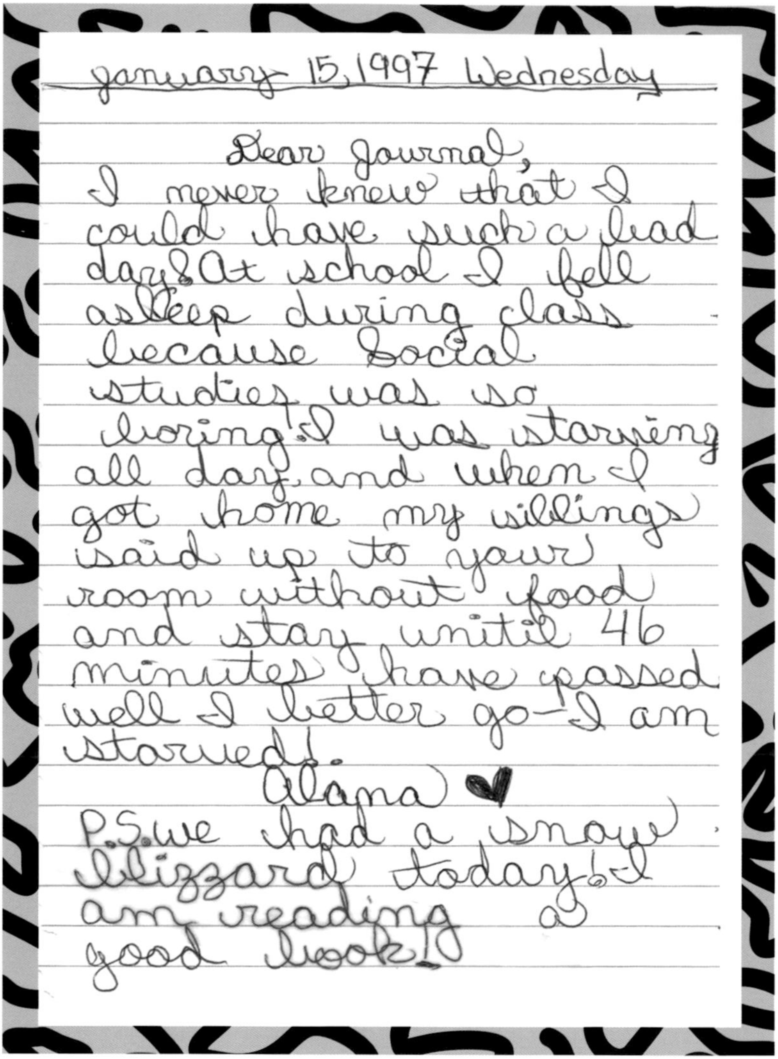

January 15, 1997 Wednesday

Dear Journal,
I never knew that I could have such a bad day. At school I fell asleep during class because Social studies was so boring. I was starving all day, and when I got home my siblings said up to your room without food and stay until 46 minutes have passed well I better go—I am starved!
Alana ♥
P.S. we had a snow blizzard today! I am reading a good book!

(Age 11)

My neighbor and I were having one last sleepover before she left for summer camp. Since my birthday is on the twentieth of June and she was leaving on the nineteenth, I decided it would also be my birthday celebration (let the big, unrealistic expectations begin). I was being super dramatic, acting like I'd never see her again and that once she came back at the end of summer, we'd somehow be too far apart in age to be friends anymore. Understandably, Rachel wanted to get to bed early since she had to pack/leave for camp the following day. When I kept harassing her about playing a board game, she decided to walk back over to her house so she could get some sleep. Clearly, I handled that well.

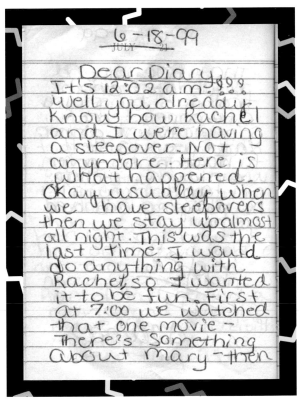

(Age 13)

Continued on next page

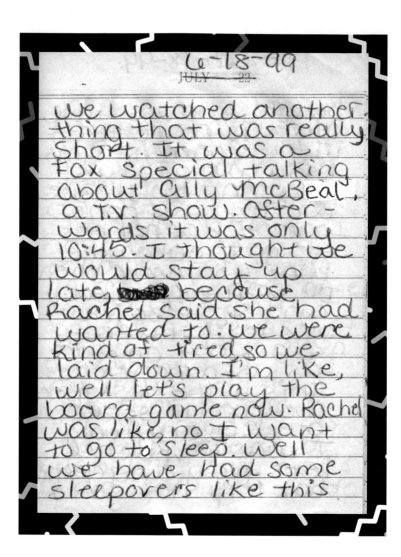

6-18-99
~~JULY 22~~

We watched another
thing that was really
short. It was a
Fox special talking
about Ally McBeal,
a T.V. show. After-
wards it was only
10:45. I thought we
would stay up
late, ~~because~~ because
Rachel said she had
wanted to. We were
kind of tired, so we
laid down. I'm like,
well let's play the
board game now. Rachel
was like, no I want
to go to sleep. Well
we have had some
sleepovers like this

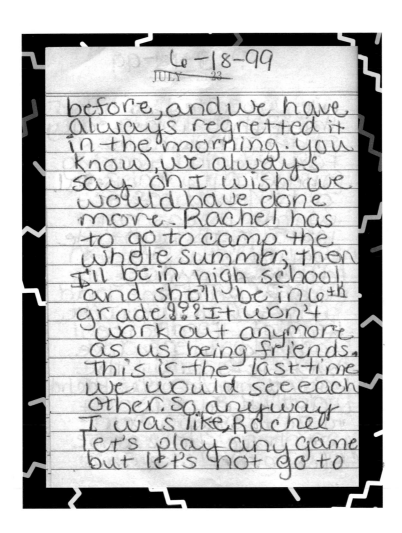

6-18-99
JULY 23

before, and we have always regretted it in the morning. you know, we always say oh I wish we would have done more. Rachel has to go to camp the whole summer, then I'll be in high school and she'll be in 6th grade??? It won't work out anymore as us being friends. This is the last time we would see each other. So anyway I was like, Rachel let's play any game but let's not go to

Continued on next page

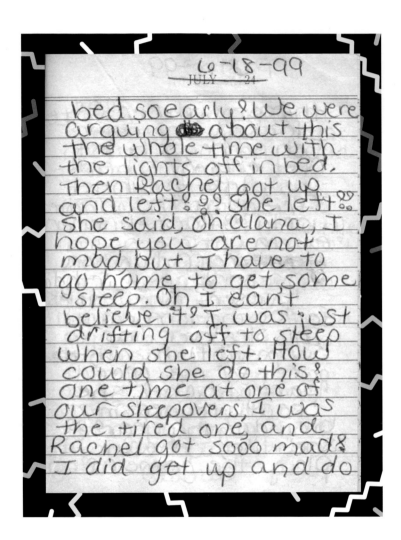

6-18-99

JULY 24

bed so early! We were
arguing about this
the whole time with
the lights off in bed.
Then Rachel got up
and left!?? She left!!
She said, Oh Alana, I
hope you are not
mad but I have to
go home to get some
sleep. Oh I can't
believe it! I was just
drifting off to sleep
when she left. How
could she do this?
one time at one of
our sleepovers, I was
the tired one, and
Rachel got sooo mad!
I did get up and do

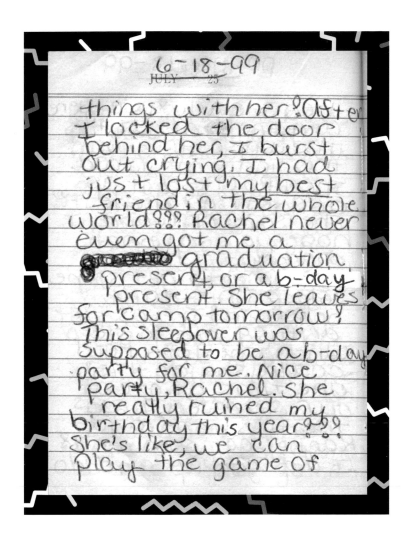

6-18-99

things with her? After I locked the door behind her, I burst out crying. I had just lost my best friend in the whole world??? Rachel never even got me a ~~graduation~~ graduation present, or a b-day present. She leaves for camp tomorrow! This sleepover was supposed to be a b-day party for me. Nice party, Rachel. She really ruined my birthday this year??? She's like, we can play the game of

Continued on next page

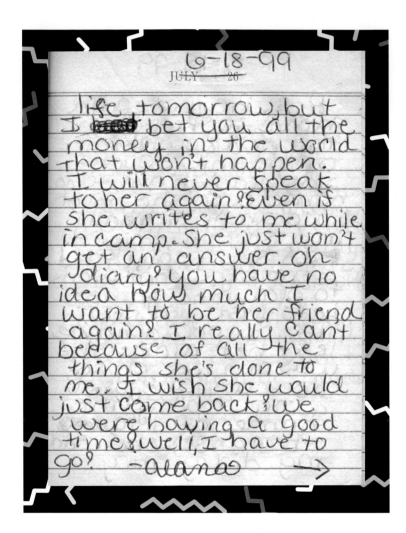

6-18-99

JULY 26

life tomorrow, but I ~~bet~~ bet you all the money in the world that won't happen. I will never speak to her again! Even if she writes to me while in camp. She just won't get an answer. oh diary! you have no idea how much I want to be her friend again! I really can't because of all the things she's done to me. I wish she would just come back! we were having a good time! Well, I have to go! -alana →

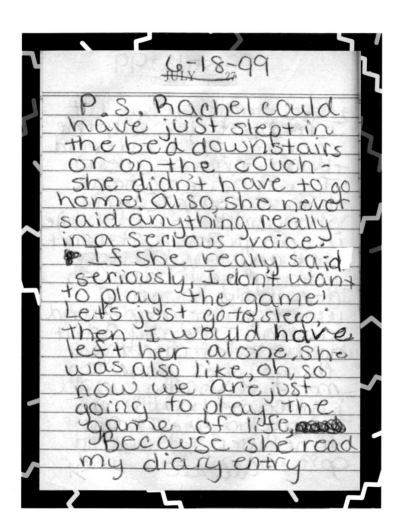

6-18-99
~~JULY 27~~

P.S. Rachel could
have just slept in
the bed downstairs
or on the couch -
she didn't have to go
home! Also, she never
said anything really
in a serious voice,
If she really said
seriously, I don't want
to play the game!
Let's just go to sleep,
Then I would have
left her alone, she
was also like, oh, so
now we are just
going to play the
game of life,
Because she read
my diary entry

Continued on next page

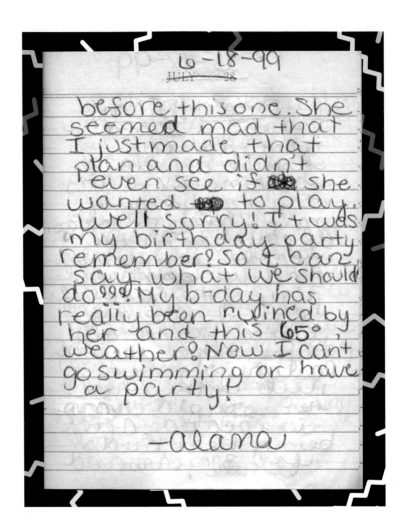

6-18-99
JULY 28

before this one. She seemed mad that I just made that plan and didn't even see if she wanted to play. Well sorry! It was my birthday party remember? So I can say what we should do??? My b-day has really been ruined by her and this 65°, weather! Now I can't go swimming or have a party!

-alana

I was consumed by jealousy and rage when I found out Rachel was actually having fun at camp. After reading her most recent letter that said she was taking a dance class but wasn't fond of jazz (which was my favorite), I decided we had absolutely nothing in common anymore and simply could not be friends.

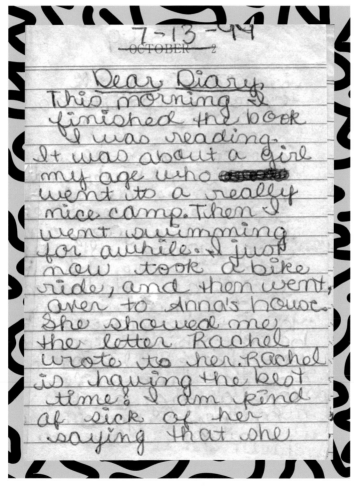

(Age 14)

Continued on next page

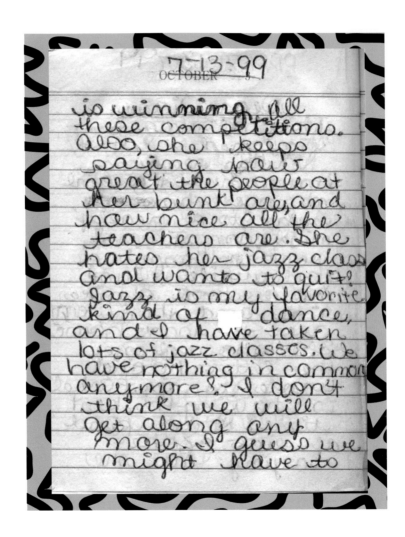

7-13-99
OCTOBER 99

is winning all
these competitions.
Also, she keeps
saying how
great the people at
her bunk are, and
how nice all the
teachers are. She
hates her jazz class
and wants to quit!
Jazz is my favorite
kind of   dance,
and I have taken
lots of jazz classes. We
have nothing in common
anymore! I don't
think we will
get along any
more. I guess we
might have to

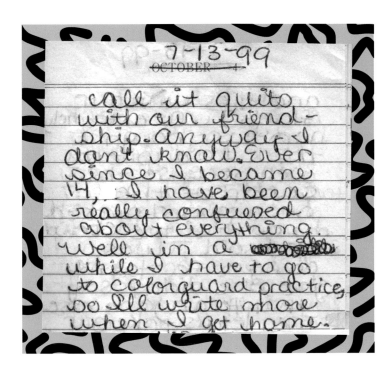

7-13-99
~~OCTOBER~~

call it quits
with our friend-
ship. Anyway I
don't know. Ever
since I became
14, I have been
really confused
about everything.
Well in a ~~whole~~
while I have to go
to colorguard practice,
so I'll write more
when I get home.

Chapter Five

Artwork, Poetry, and Lisa Frank

PART ONE
ARTWORK

Before cell phones, iPads, social media, and anything else kids do these days for entertainment, our options back in the nineties consisted of playing Super Nintendo, watching Nickelodeon, or playing outside. When those got boring, I either wrote in my diary or did art projects. Although I was terrible at drawing, I absolutely loved making "artwork." Once I realized that I was pretty limited on what I was able to draw, I resorted to the only things I was capable of creating while still being recognizable— i.e., balloons, rainbows, and flowers. I was super excited when Crayola came out with new types of markers or crayons and could hardly wait to get my hands on them.

Anytime there was a bunch of white space, I got out my stamp markers and went to town.

My attempt at painting. I used a big glob of sparkly gold glitter glue for the sun.

Once I mastered balloons, I moved on to rainbows.

I created this masterpiece with my new glitter crayons.

Those are some extremely tall flowers. Once my yellow marker
touched those black sunglasses it was all over.

I really went all out for this one.

I painted balloons and decided to jazz them
up a bit with some Lisa Frank stickers.

One of my favorite Christmas presents was when my mom bought us Crayola Marker Airbrush. You simply inserted a marker into the airbrush device, picked out a stencil, and went to work. For added effect, I decided to use some stick-on earrings.

This cat would've been pretty cool if I hadn't drawn such a creepy face on it.

This paint-blob art required the least amount of effort,
yet looks the best.

Trying out my new wacky tip markers and Lisa Frank sticker tape.

When I was in fourth grade in 1994, we made a memory book for our parents. Part of that project involved answering the question, "If you could find anything at the end of the rainbow, what would it be?" We then had to draw a picture of the items we chose. After weighing the options carefully of what was most important to me, I chose three things: $10,000,000, gold, and a puppy. As you can see, drawing animals wasn't my strong suit.

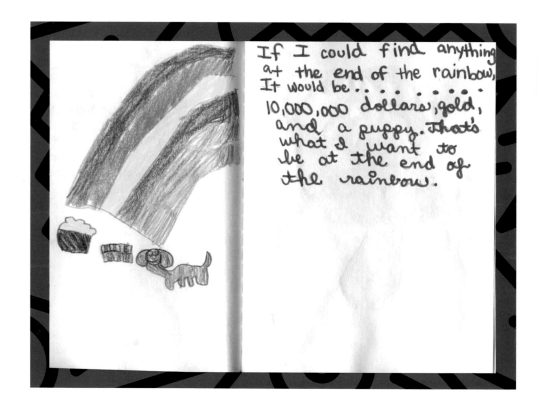

PART TWO
POETRY

After learning about poetry in sixth grade, our teacher thought it would be nice if each student wrote a poetry book to give to their mom for Mother's Day. I didn't feel particularly skilled in that area, but gave it my best shot.

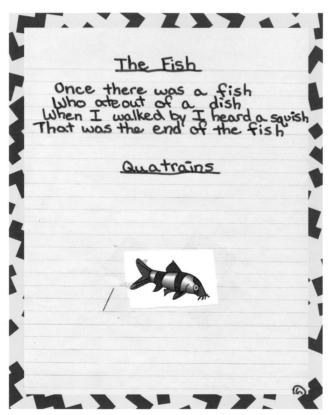

After writing my book of poems and trying to figure out
which one should be first, I felt the one about killing a fish
would be appropriate.

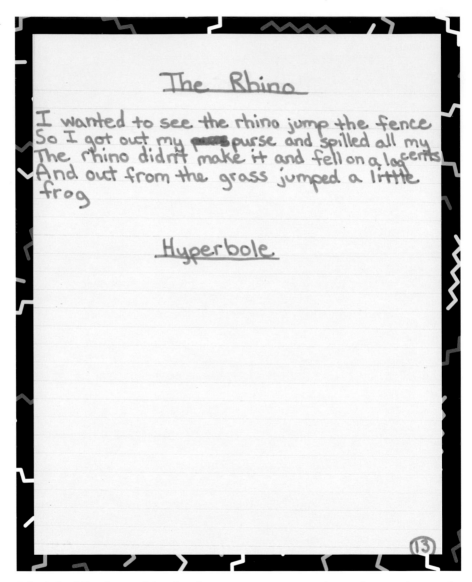

The Rhino

I wanted to see the rhino jump the fence
So I got out my ~~purse~~ purse and spilled all my
The rhino didn't make it and fell on a lacerts
And out from the grass jumped a little
frog

Hyperbole

⑬

I don't think I understood that there's more to writing poetry than picking random words that rhyme—it should also make sense.

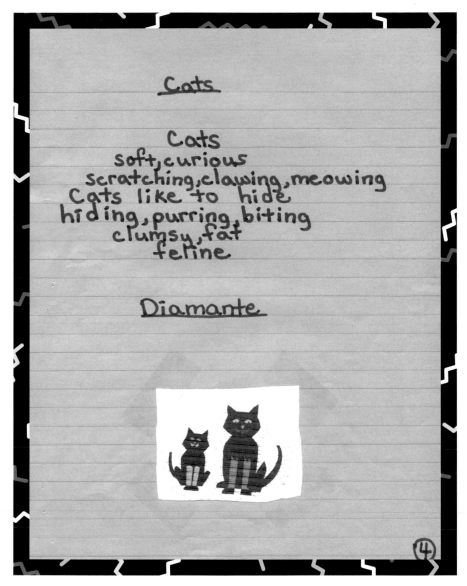

Cats

Cats
soft, curious
scratching, clawing, meowing
Cats like to hide
hiding, purring, biting
clumsy, fat
feline

Diamante

When thinking about how to describe cats, words like scratching, clawing, biting, clumsy, and fat came to mind.

Ducky

I was so bored
but then I got lucky
Out popped a little ducky

Triplet

I'm sure my mom was impressed by the amount of time and effort it took me to create this poem.

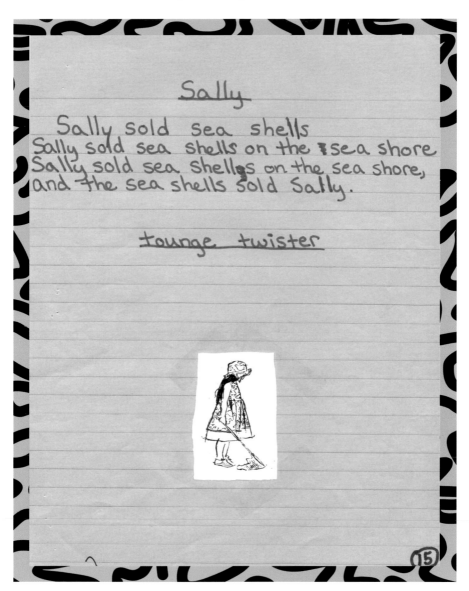

Sally

Sally sold sea shells
Sally sold sea shells on the sea shore
Sally sold sea shells on the sea shore,
and the sea shells sold Sally.

tounge twister

The classic *Sally Sold Sea Shells by the Sea Shore* tongue twister, but with a surprise ending.

PART THREE
LISA FRANK

Saying that I was obsessed with Lisa Frank as a child would be an understatement. I absolutely lived for those little stationery sets that included stickers, envelopes, stationery, and a really awesome pen. Nothing made me happier than opening a present and catching a glimpse of one of her bold, colorful designs hiding under the tissue paper.

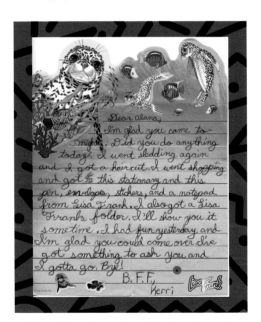

My best friend was also a Lisa Frank junkie, so whenever one of us received new items, it was a big deal and required writing a note.

When coloring in my Lisa Frank coloring book, I tried to mimic her style by incorporating rainbow colors wherever possible.

I treasured my Lisa Frank stickers so much that I didn't even want to use them.

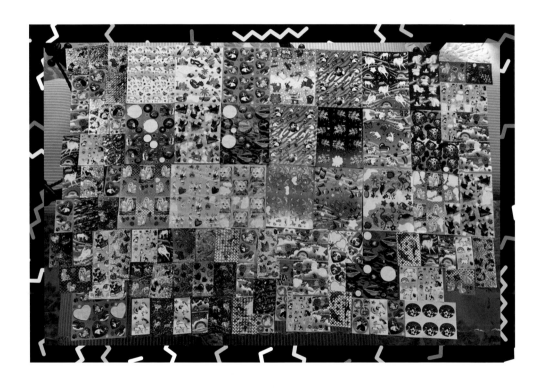

I still can't let go of these prized possessions.

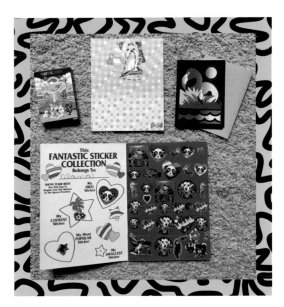

Chapter Six

Dear Mom

Photobombing started early for me.

When visiting my parents' house several months ago, my mom informed me that I had written her several notes when I was younger. The majority of them were written on Saturday nights when my parents went to a restaurant called The Woodcutter for dinner and dancing. It provided me with the perfect opportunity to get out my favorite Lisa Frank stationery and write a note for my mom to find once she returned. The notes had been tucked away in her bedroom closet for nearly twenty years and she had recently discovered them while cleaning. My quick afternoon visit turned into hours of reminiscing, laughing, and telling stories about the past.

(Age 10)

Nothing says "Happy Easter!" like a remote control to the head. After asking my mom for forgiveness, I tried to suck up by offering her sweet tarts.

I gave my mom a heads-up about possibly having to go to the principal's office, but decided to hold off on the explanation.

Dear Mommy,
Did your read the other letter I wrote you? Well tonight or tommorrow I will tell you why I might have to go to the principle's office. When you are back I'm probubly still awake. I can't really fall asleep. Did you have a good time at the woodcutter? You might want to go to sleep after a long day. Are we going to open swim tommorrow? Because it is really fun there. Maybe we can go to the mall today. Or maybe another day if you don't feel up to it. Tonight we watched some of Batman Forever. Then we pushed stop, went up stairs, and tried to go to bed. I had a good time at Chelseas house. Goodnight! Love always, Alana

(Age 10)

It completely blew my mind that my feet were the same size as my sister's, who was five years older, and I felt compelled to write my mom a note about it. I also needed her approval on my Lisa Frank stationery.

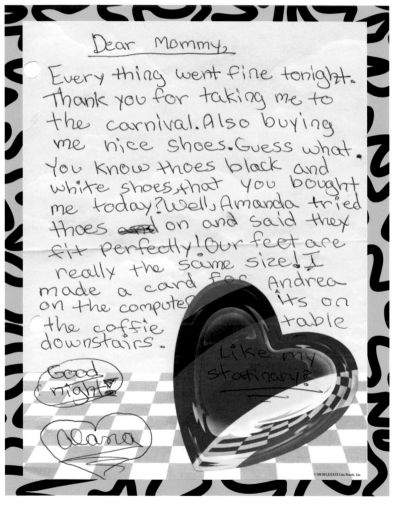

(Age 10)

At a young age, I attempted to be the mediator of the family. I felt that I should be the one to talk to my brother about keeping his room clean. After thinking about it a bit more, I decided room cleanliness was such a serious matter that it required help from a psychiatrist.

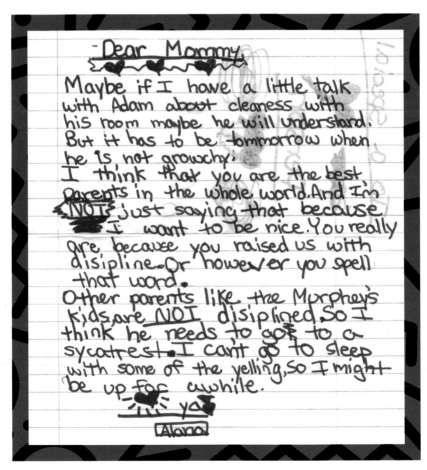

(Age 10)

(Age 11)

It's always a good idea to start off a note to your mom by confronting her about something. Of course, me being aggravating was all just hearsay. Once again, I warned my mom about having to go to the principal's office, but spared her the details until a more appropriate time. I have a feeling I never received French toast the next morning.

I needed to remind my mom that she had yet to buy me a birthday present.

7-4-98

Dear Mom,

After I read thoes letters I wrote you, I felt like writing one now. So, this summer has gone bye soooo fast! Tomorrow is Saturday, so maybe you and I can go shopping. You still haven't gotten me a birthday present yet, ya know! Well today, Kerri and I had a really fun time at the pool. We held each other up by our hands and then flipped the person into a backward flip. Anyway, after that, when I went to her house at 7:00, she had some of her own fireworks that we set off with the help of her dad. Then we went to see the firework show downtown, which was basically the same as every past year. Well, try to write back sometime!

Love always,
♡Alana♡

(Age 13)

I apologized to my mom for not doing my chores and then tried to butter her up by giving her a bottle of used perfume I had found in my bedroom.

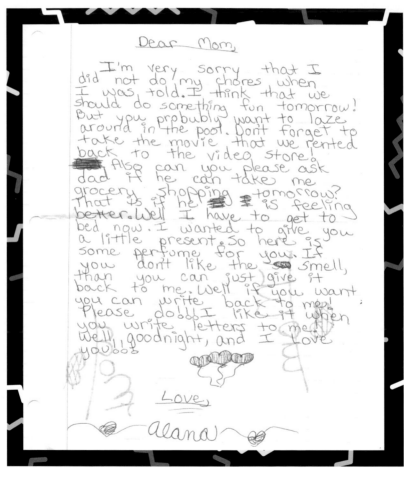

(Age 11)

Talk about bombarding her with questions, sheesh.

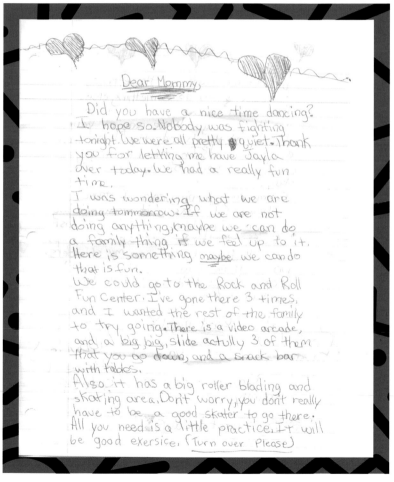

Dear Mommy,

Did you have a nice time dancing? I hope so. Nobody was fighting tonight. We were all pretty quiet. Thank you for letting me have Jayla over today. We had a really fun time.

I was wondering what we are doing tommorow. If we are not doing anything, maybe we can do a family thing if we feel up to it. Here is something maybe we can do that is fun.

We could go to the Rock and Roll Fun Center. I've gone there 3 times, and I wanted the rest of the family to try going. There is a video arcade, and a big big, slide actully 3 of them that you go down, and a snack bar with tables.

Also it has a big roller blading and skating area. Don't worry, you don't really have to be a good skater to go there. All you need is a little practice. It will be good exersice. (Turn over Please)

(Age 11)

Continued on next page

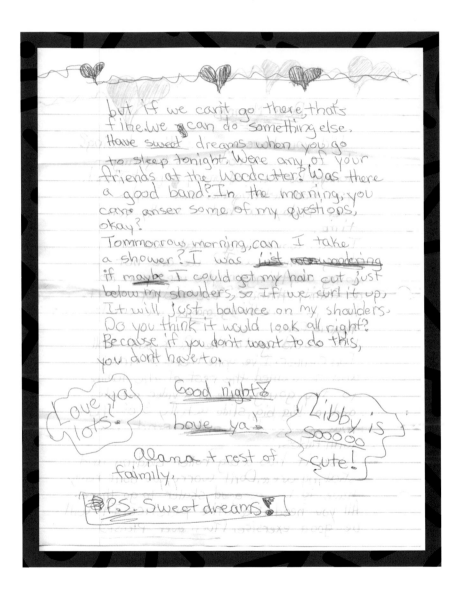

but if we can't go there, that's fine. We can do something else. Have sweet dreams when you go to sleep tonight. Were any of your friends at the Woodcutter? Was there a good band? In the morning, you can anser some of my questions, okay?

Tommorrow morning, can I take a shower? I was ~~just was wondering~~ if maybe I could get my hair cut just below my shoulders, so if we curl it up, it will just balance on my shoulders. Do you think it would look all right? Because if you don't want to do this, you don't have to.

Good night

Love ya
lots.

Love ya!

Libby is sooooo cute!

Alana + rest of faimly.

P.S. Sweet dreams!

When you're watching television as a kid and you see someone with the same first and last name as one of your sister's friends, it's a big deal.

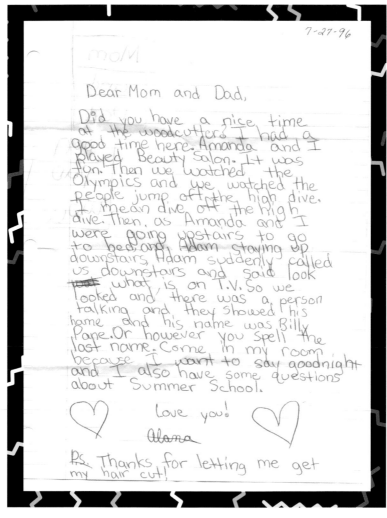

7-27-96

mom

Dear Mom and Dad,

Did you have a nice time at the woodcutters? I had a good time here. Amanda and I played Beauty Salon. It was fun. Then we watched the Olympics and we watched the people jump off the high dive. I mean dive off the high dive. Then, as Amanda and I were going upstairs to go to bed and Adam staying up downstairs, Adam suddenly called us downstairs and said look what is on T.V. So we looked and there was a person talking and they showed his name and his name was Billy Pane. Or however you spell the last name. Come in my room because I want to say goodnight and I also have some questions about Summer School.

Love you!
Alana

P.S. Thanks for letting me get my hair cut!

(Age 11)

Chapter Seven

Homework Fails

I heard the background for this school photo was going
to be paint splatter, and I conveniently owned a pair of
paint-splattered overalls.

While searching for old diaries, I was surprised to find that I had also kept several note-books from school. Not thinking I would find anything interesting in them, they were almost completely set aside and forgotten about until I randomly decided to flip through them one day—and thank goodness I did. In this chapter, I share with you some of my favorite home-work fails.

Well, that's a perfectly logical reason for not wanting to be a famous athlete. Apparently, I couldn't think of a single person in my life who I was proud of.

In sixth grade, you weren't one of the cool girls unless you were reading Lurlene McDaniel books. Looking back on it, I'm not exactly sure why these extremely depressing books were so popular, but I jumped on the bandwagon and got hooked. As a homework assignment, our class was asked to write letters to the teacher in order to keep her up to speed on books we were reading.

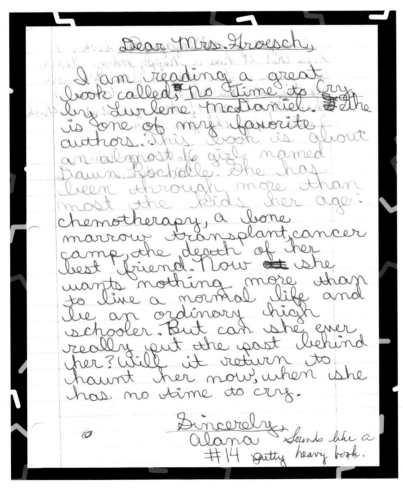

Dear Mrs. Hroesch,

I am reading a great book called; "No Time to Cry" by Lurlene McDaniel. The is one of my favorite authors. This book is about an almost 16 girl named Dawn Rochelle. She has been through more than most the kids her age: chemotherapy, a bone marrow transplant, cancer camp, the death of her best friend. Now she wants nothing more than to live a normal life and be an ordinary high schooler. But can she ever really put the past behind her? Will it return to haunt her now, when she has no time to cry.

Sincerely,
Alana
#14

Sounds like a pretty heavy book.

(Age 12)

Instead of summarizing the book in my own words, I took the easy way out and copied it straight from the back of the book. Luckily, my teacher didn't seem to mind.

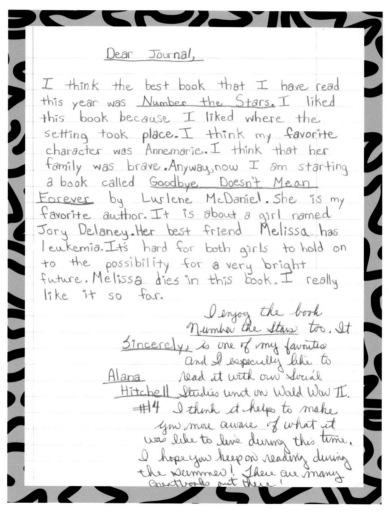

Dear Journal,

I think the best book that I have read this year was Number the Stars. I liked this book because I liked where the setting took place. I think my favorite character was Annemarie. I think that her family was brave. Anyway, now I am starting a book called Goodbye, Doesn't Mean Forever by Lurlene McDaniel. She is my favorite author. It is about a girl named Jory Delaney. Her best friend Melissa has leukemia. It's hard for both girls to hold on to the possibility for a very bright future. Melissa dies in this book. I really like it so far.

Sincerely,

Alana Hitchell #14

I enjoy the book Number the Stars too. It is one of my favorites and I especially like to read it with our Social Studies unit on World War II. I think it helps to make you more aware of what it was like to live during this time. I hope you keep on reading during the summer! There are many great books out there!

(Age 12)

At least I only plagiarized a couple of sentences this time. The fact that one of the main characters ends up dying didn't seem to faze me.

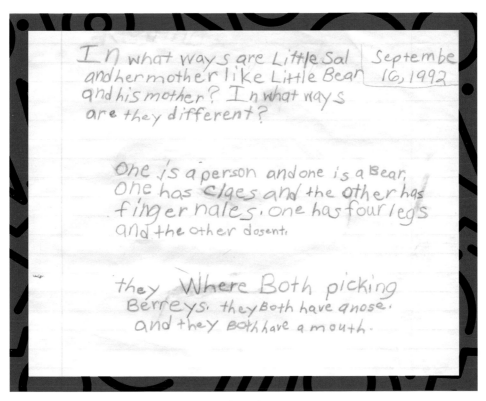

In what ways are Little Sal and her mother like Little Bear and his mother? In what ways are they different?

September 16, 1992

One is a person and one is a Bear. One has claes and the other has finger nales. one has four legs and the other dosent.

they Where Both picking Berreys. they Both have a nose. and they Both have a mouth.

(Age 7)

I have a feeling that when my teacher asked for a character comparison she was referring to personality traits and not, "They both have a nose and they both have a mouth."

Before our class started reading *Stone Fox*, we were asked to predict what the book was about based on the cover alone. We were not allowed to look at the back of the book or flip through it. Mysteriously, I correctly predicted one of the main character's names.

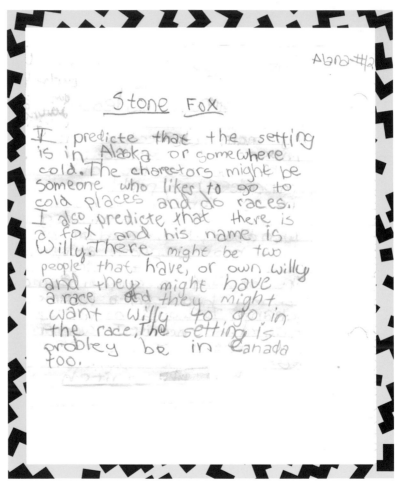

(Age 8)

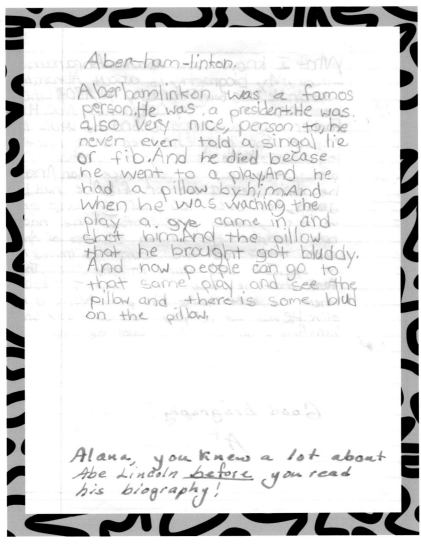

Aber-ham-linkon.

Aberhamlinkon was a famos person. He was a president. He was also very nice, person to, he never ever told a singal lie or fib. And he died becase he went to a play, And he had a pillow by him. And when he was waching the play a. gye came in and shot him. And the pillow that he brought got bluddy. And now people can go to that same play and see the pillow and there is some blud on the pillow.

Alana, you knew a lot about Abe Lincoln _before_ you read his biography!

(Age 7)

I have some doubts that I actually knew this much information about "Aber-ham-linkon" before reading his biography. Evidently, so did my teacher.

As you can see from the following examples, social studies wasn't my best subject.

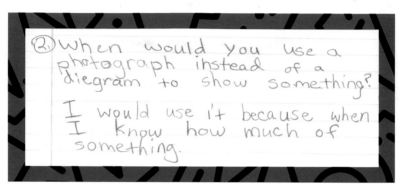

2) When would you use a photograph instead of a diegram to show something?

I would use it because when I know how much of something.

7) It's in the middel of the region because it has farms, and a lot of other stuff.

1) Why are deltas usally good for farming?
Deltas are good for farming because they help good.

2) What is the difference between a river and a lake?
a river is a long body of water and a lake is a big bodie of water, and it is deep.

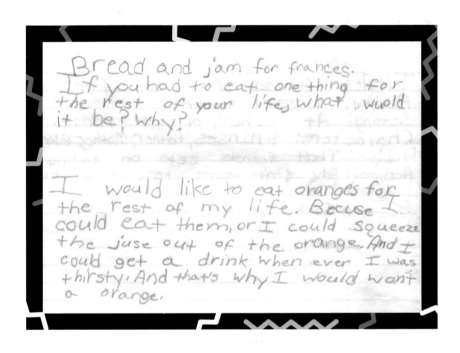

Bread and jam for frances.
If you had to eat one thing for
the rest of your life, what wuold
it be? why?

I would like to eat oranges for
the rest of my life. Becuse I
could eat them, or I could squeeze
the juse out of the orange. And I
could get a drink when ever I was
thirsty. And that's why I would want
a orange.

Most second graders would probably choose their favorite kind of junk food. However, I was thinking more along the lines of survival, so I chose oranges.

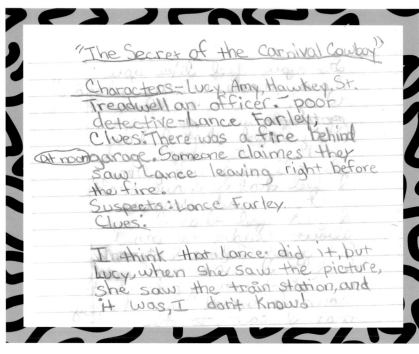

"The Secret of the Carnival Cowboy"

Characters- Lucy, Amy, Hawkey, St. Treadwell an officer. poor detective-Lance Farley,

Clues: There was a fire behind garage. Someone claimes they saw Lance leaving right before the fire.

At noon

Suspects: Lance Farley.

Clues:

I think that Lance did it, but Lucy, when she saw the picture, she saw the train station, and it was, I don't know!

(Age 11)

When making my prediction about who started the fire, I seemed to get a bit frazzled.

On how watching television affects young children:

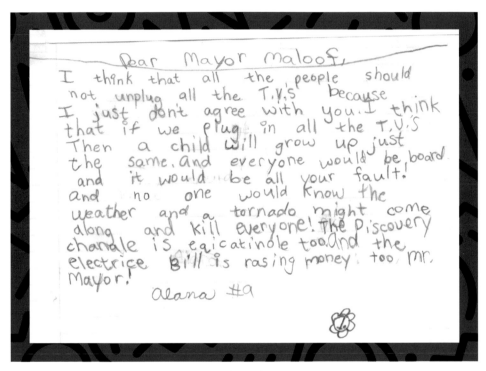

Dear Mayor maloof,
I think that all the people should
not unplug all the T.V.'s because
I just don't agree with you. I think
that if we plug in all the T.V.'s
Then a child will grow up just
the same. And everyone would be board
and it would be all your fault!
and no one would know the
weather and a tornado might come
along and kill everyone! The Discovery
chandle is eqicatinole too. And the
electrice Bill is rasing money. too. mr.
Mayor!
          alana #9

(Age 9)

Why was I yelling at the Mayor? I really hope this wasn't some sort of rough draft and we actually sent these letters to him. I've had many spelling fails so far, but "eqicatinole" (educational) definitely takes the cake.

Chapter Eight

Aspiring Teacher and Writing Stories

In 20 years from now I would like to be a teacher. I would get payed 100,000,000 dollars a second. All my students would act ~~act~~ nicely, and they would get fun fridays every week.

Unfortunately, my dream of becoming a teacher who gets paid $100,000,000 per second didn't pan out.

In third grade, everyone had a reading journal where we would read a book and then answer questions about what we read. My teacher would collect our spiral notebooks, review what we wrote, and leave a response. Reading was typically my favorite subject, so I was always eager to see my teacher's comments. It was an extra bonus when she drew her signature smiley face (complete with hair curl).

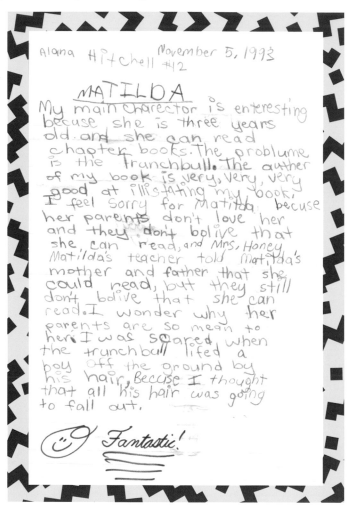

(Age 8)

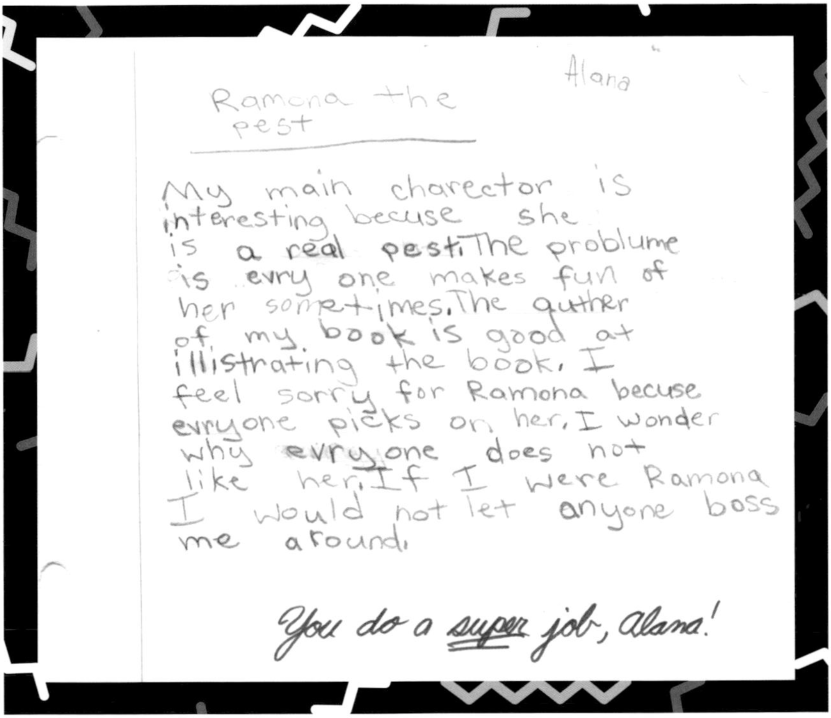

Alana

Ramona the
pest

My main charector is
interesting becuse she
is a real pesti. The problume
is evry one makes fun of
her sometimes. The guther
of my book is good at
illistrating the book, I
feel sorry for Ramona becuse
evryone picks on her, I wonder
why evryone does not
like her, If I were Ramona
I would not let anyone boss
me around.

You do a super job, Alana!

(Age 8)

Even though my spelling was awful, my teacher was always encouraging and made me feel like I was doing a great job. She even gave me an A+ for my second quarter reading grade. I was a bit disappointed, though, to see that she didn't have time to comment on every single one of my reading journal entries, so I took it upon myself to fix that problem. I found a marker that was a similar color to the one my teacher used and left comments on my own entries — pretending I was my teacher. I even tried to mimic her cursive handwriting, but was so terrible at it that my responses are barely legible. I had completely forgotten I had done this, so discovering these comments was rather amusing.

Apparently, I like to "hear about things about bees," and especially like when people get stung by them. Acting as the teacher, I wrote, "I liked the part about the bees too!"

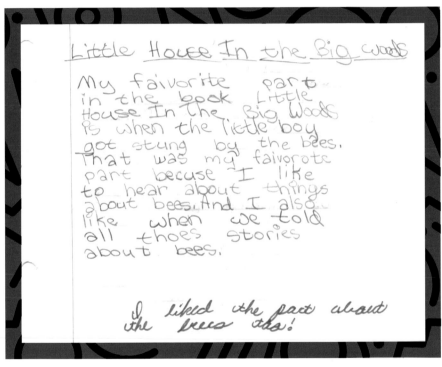

(Age 8)

Instead of summarizing a book, we were asked to write about our responsibilities around the house. I gave myself an A+ and wrote, "I bet you are that responsible around your house. You seem to be really responsible at school also!"

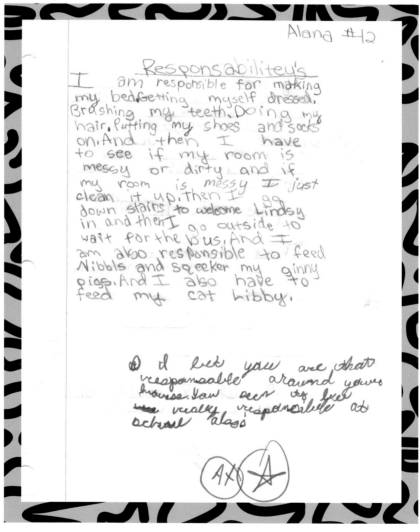

(Age 8)

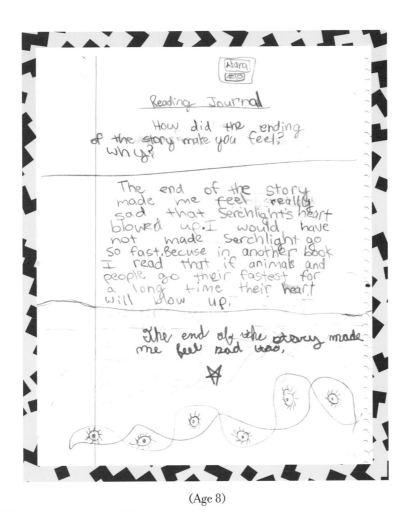

(Age 8)

Why on Earth were we reading a book about a dog whose heart blows up? That seems a bit much for third graders to handle.

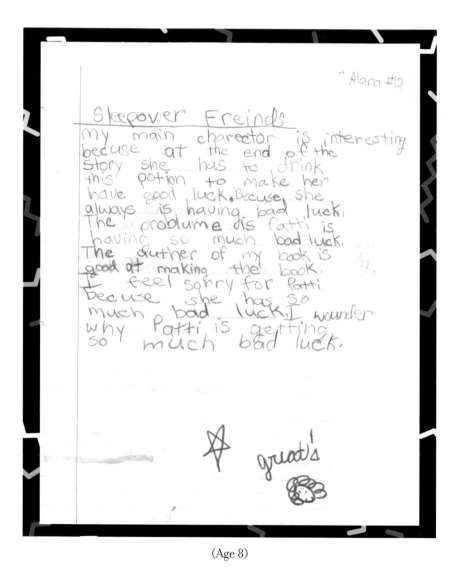

" Alana #12

Sleepover Freinds
My main charector is interesting
becuse at the end of the
story she has to drink
this potion to make her
have good luck. Becuse she
always is having bad luck,
The problume is Patti is
having so much bad luck,
The auther of my book is
good at making the book,
I feel sorry for Patti
becuse she has so
much bad luck. I wounder
why Patti is getting
so much bad luck.

great's

(Age 8)

Although I told myself I did great, I don't think I was clear enough about how the main character has bad luck.

Near the beginning of third grade, my two front teeth were forcefully knocked out by someone's elbow on the school bus. I'm assuming the force of them being knocked out when they weren't ready had something to do with my adult teeth never coming in on their own. When I still didn't have front teeth a year and a half later near the end of fourth grade, my mom finally decided it was time to do something about it. My gums were very rough at that point. I could feel the teeth in there, but for some reason they just couldn't break through. I'm not sure the procedure really constitutes as having surgery, but when I asked my mom what the dentist was going to do, she didn't sugarcoat it— he was going to cut my gums open. I imagine the kids at school must have been pretty confused when I suddenly showed up with teeth, so I decided to write a paper about it.

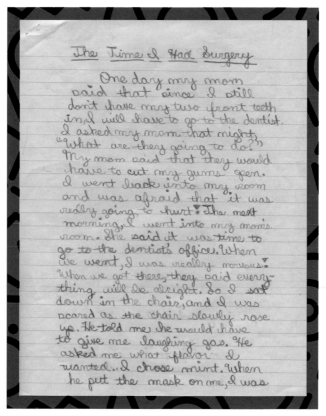

(Age 9)

Continued on next page

scared. I really wanted to go home.
I started to drift away like what
seemed into space. I felt like I
was spinning around and around
in blackness. Then, it seemed like I
hit space and was walking around
on the moon. Then all of the
sudden a little bee came
out of nowhere, and stung
me right on my gums. The bee
stung me for a long time, and
then he flew away. I had really
sore gums. Then I tripped over
a dip in space and fell on
my back. I fell asleep for a
long time and when I woke up,
there was a dentist in front
of me. "ALL DONE!" he shouted
in a loud booming voice. I got up
and slowly left the dentist's
office with my mom.
     That night I kept on spitting
out blood. My mom was a
little worried. Then I had to
go back to the dentist's office

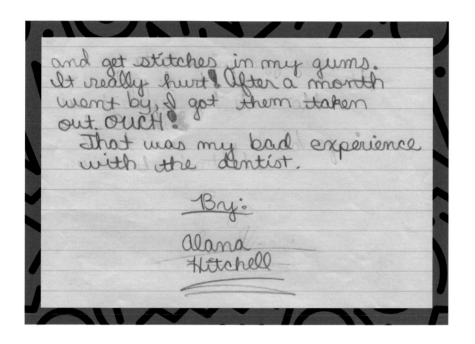

and get stitches in my gums.
It really hurt! After a month
went by, I got them taken
out. OUCH!

That was my bad experience
with the dentist.

By:

Alana
Hitchell

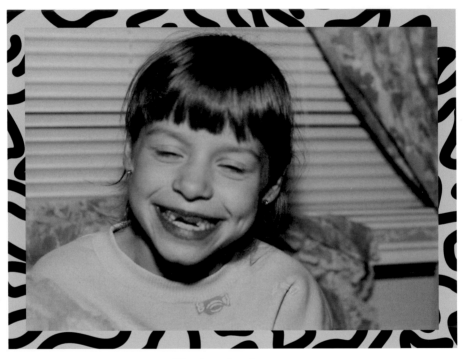

Here's a nice close-up.

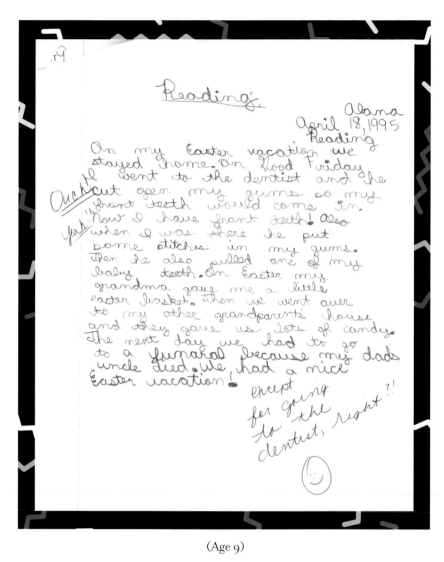

(Age 9)

Even though I went to a funeral, had my gums cut open, stitches put in the roof of my mouth, and had a tooth pulled, I still considered it a nice Easter vacation.

In fifth grade around Halloween, we were asked to write a story about a time we were scared. My teacher was probably thinking we'd write about being scared of things like spiders, the dark, etc. I don't think she was expecting me to write about the time a drunken man tried to grab my brother while we were on vacation.

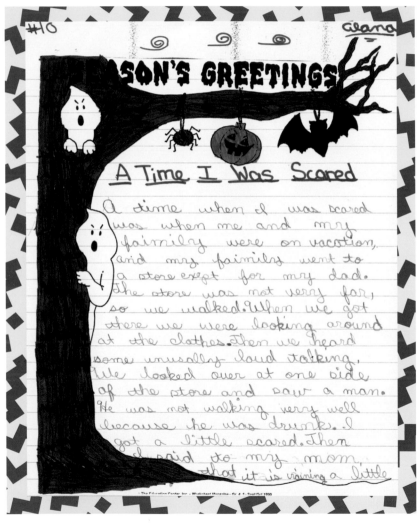

(Age 10)

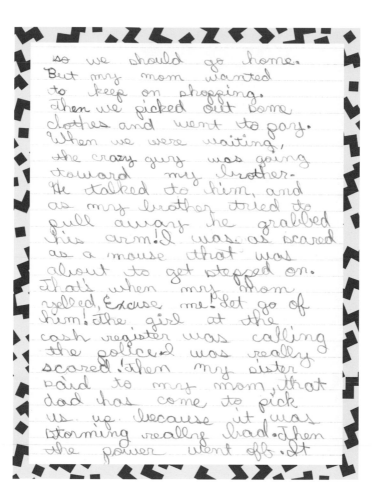

so we should go home.
But my mom wanted
to keep on shopping.
Then we picked out some
clothes and went to pay.
When we were waiting,
the crazy guy was going
toward my brother.
He talked to him, and
as my brother tried to
pull away he grabbed
his arm! I was as scared
as a mouse that was
about to get stepped on.
That's when my mom
yelled, Excuse me! Let go of
him! The girl at the
cash register was calling
the police. I was really
scared! Then my sister
said to my mom, that
dad has come to pick
us up because it was
storming really bad. Then
the power went off. It

Continued on next page

was all dark in the store.
We ran to our van but
had to wait because the
doors were locked and the
power was off. My mom
was still waiting in
the store to pay. When
we got inside our van,
I was as wet as a
drowned rat. Then I looked
out my window and saw
that the police had come
and took the drunk person
away. The next day we
went strait home. That
was a really scary night!

Alana
Mitchell
10-20-95

Reading *A Time I Was Scared* to my classmates. I even brought in props: the sweatshirt I purchased at the store from my story, and a flashlight to indicate the store's power being off.

One of my favorite school subjects was creative writing. It's apparent from the following stories I wrote in third grade that getting close to the bottom of the page required ending the story abruptly instead of simply turning the page over to continue writing.

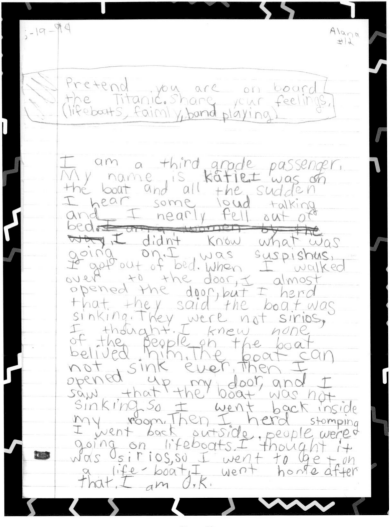

(Age 8)

November 17, 1993

my name is Henry.
and I'm a turkey.
My owner's name is Bob.
and one day he gave
me this big dinner, And
I knew he was up to
some thing, so he cept kept
on letting me eat all
of his food. So one day
I said I was ready
to eat my big dinner,
and then I knew that he
wanted to kill me and eat
me for Thanksgiving. So when
he went upstairs then I
did not eat my dinner, I
threw my dinner away and
then my owner came and
asked me if I ate my dinner
and I said yes. And so thanksgiving came and I looked in
his room, one knight, and
I saw him with a big knife!
So I ran downstars, and my
owner came down and wanted
to kill me for Thanksgiving,
So he got his knife and started
coming at me. and soon he baked
me up in a wall and I said,
"I thought you were my
freind. So he said that he was my
freind so we lived happily ever
after. me end

(Age 8)

Chapter Nine

Awkward Christmas Photos

I just look plain scary.

Our family always had the best Christmas celebrations. We received tons of presents, stuffed ourselves with Christmas cookies, and played hours upon hours of Super Nintendo. My least favorite part of Christmas was the dreaded Christmas card photo. My mom would pose us super awkwardly, continuously adjust our hair/clothing, and then get stressed out when the perfect image she had in her head wasn't translating into reality. We just couldn't seem to get it right. In fact, our Christmas card photo issues date all the way back to the late eighties when I was just a baby. Here are some examples of when I ruined every single picture.

About to sneeze.

Sleeping.

Looking unhappy/bow slipping off head.

Crying.

Stressed out.

Possibly going potty.

Finally, a good one! My siblings look like they've had enough.

Instead of looking happy and natural, my mom preferred us to be super serious.

Still going for the serious vibe a year later.

I was supposed to act like I was handing
the present up to my siblings but ended up
looking incredibly awkward.

My mom thought an outdoor Christmas photo
might be nice, but this was the result.

Maybe facing a different direction would help—nope.

My mom then decided to move us
inside on the staircase, but that didn't
seem to work either.

She ended up choosing this lovely photo for our Christmas card that was sent out to about fifty of our friends and family members. I was teased for years about my awkward head tilt.

The Hitchells 1993

May your days be Merry & Bright!

Amanda 13, Adam 10, Alana 8

I was given strict instructions to pretend I
was admiring an ornament on the tree.

As we got older, the photos kept getting worse.

I mean, wow.

We finally decided to stand around the piano
and call it a day.

My sister's face says it all.

Chapter Ten

'90s Nostalgia

My siblings and I wearing our classic '90s coats.

That is one creepy doll.

Oh, how I miss the nineties. There will never be another decade like it. I was five years old in the year 1990, which, in my opinion, is the best age you could possibly be when entering this magical decade. I was old enough to have actual memories, yet young enough to have had my entire childhood ahead of me. There was just the right amount of technology. The Internet hadn't yet taken over the world; it was merely a place to do research, check out cool websites, and send emails. Instead of checking Facebook to see what was going on in your friend's life, you had to actually call them on the phone or stop by their house. If it was their birthday, you gave them a gift or sent a birthday card as opposed to a text or social media message. Those sorts of things seemed much more personalized and meaningful. It was a more innocent time when songs on the radio and movies were censored appropriately for children, unlike today where it seems like anything goes. What I probably miss most about the decade would have to be its music and movies. People might think I'm a total weirdo, but the only movies I seem to reach for are ones from the nineties. I watch the same ones over and over again. (I don't think I've been to an actual movie theater in about a year.) As far as the music goes, there was such variety, and many different genres of music were considered mainstream. There seemed to be almost equal amounts of people who liked rock, rap, alternative, pop, etc. versus today where it seems to be one big genre of pop and all the others have somewhat faded away. I could go on forever about this topic, but I digress. In a nutshell, the nineties were incredible, and I couldn't write this book without including some of my fondest memories and moments that I'll never forget.

TIME WITH GRANDPARENTS

I'm extremely thankful to have had such wonderful grandparents growing up. At the time, I just assumed all grandparents were like mine. Not until I was much older did I realize how fortunate I truly was to have them in my life. From helping raise me and my siblings when we were babies to being involved in our school activities, they were always there for us. One of my favorite memories was Grandparents Day when they would spend the day with me at school. I remember feeling super special and loved because I was one of the only students in my class who had all four grandparents come. Most of my classmates had at least one grandparent who either didn't live nearby, was in a nursing home, or had passed away. My best friend didn't have any grandparents who were able to make it to Grandparents Day, so one set of mine decided to eat lunch with her and follow her around for some of the day so that she wouldn't feel left out.

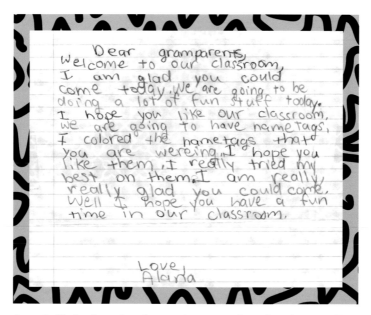

Dear gramparents,
Welcome to our classroom,
I am glad you could
come today. We are going to be
doing a lot of fun stuff today.
I hope you like our classroom,
we are going to have name tags,
I colored the name tags that
you are wereing. I hope you
like them, I really tried my
best on them. I am really
really glad you could come.
Well I hope you have a fun
time in our classroom.

Love,
Alaina

I was thrilled to have found not only pictures from Grandparents Day,
but also the note I wrote to them when they arrived at my school.

GRANDPARENTS DAY

Me with Grandma and Grandpa Day.

Me with Grandma and Grandpa Hitchell. I don't think we were quite ready for the photo.

PLAYING OUTSIDE

Summertime was always my favorite season growing up—school was out, I could start planning my birthday party, and I absolutely loved spending time outdoors. There were so many fun activities we could do in the comfort of our own backyard: camping, badminton, Slip'N Slide, basketball, jumping on the trampoline, exploring in the woods, or swimming in our above-ground pool. With no real responsibilities to worry about, we would spend the entire day, from sun-up to sun-down, playing outside. Here are a few of my favorite nineties summer photos.

We'd get all the neighborhood kids together and run through the sprinkler.

Having a blast in the pool.

Party in the hot tub.

Slip'N Slide fun.

My brother and I, exhausted after a long summer day.

I made this to-do list in 1994. I miss the days of doing what you *want* to do instead of what you *have* to do.

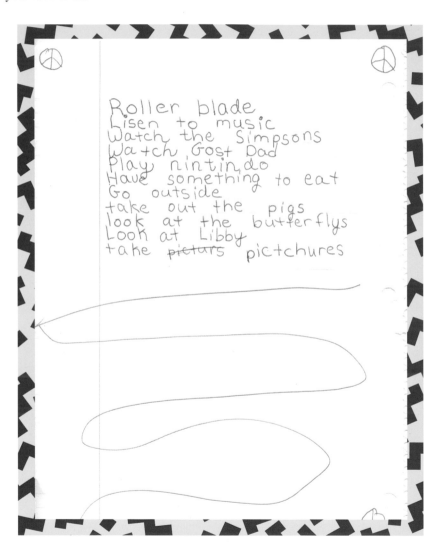

SLEEPOVERS WITH FRIENDS

I get really nostalgic when thinking about childhood sleepovers. Although some didn't exactly go as planned, the majority of them were an absolute blast. We'd stay up until four or five in the morning playing games, eating snacks, watching movies, etc. Time seemed to go by much slower back then. Hanging out with friends was ridiculously easy. You asked your friend to come over and as soon as they had a parent available to drive them, they were at your house. Sometimes I'd spend the entire day, night, and the following day with the same friend. Making plans with friends becomes far more complicated with age, especially once marriage and kids are involved. The waiting period to see one of my friends these days is at least a week. Although I had many childhood disagreements with my two best friends, Rachel and Kerri, they are both wonderful people and I'm extremely lucky to have had them in my life.

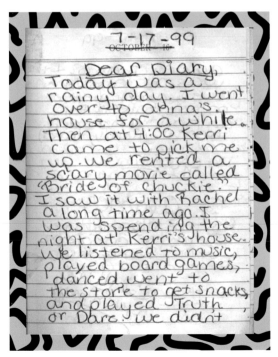

Continued on next page

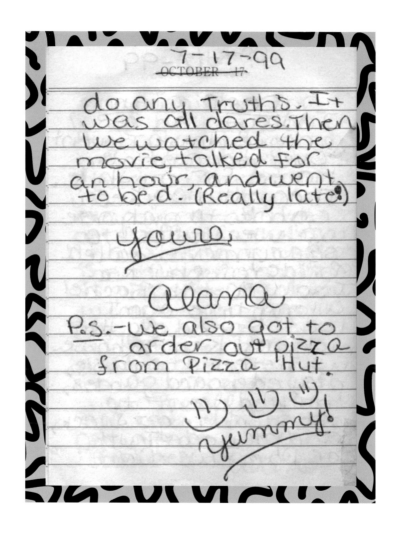

7-17-99
~~OCTOBER 17~~

do any Truths. It was all dares. Then we watched the movie, talked for an hour, and went to bed. (Really late!)

yours,

Alana

P.S. -We also got to order our pizza from Pizza Hut.

Yummy!

TAKING DANCE CLASSES

Another one of my favorite memories would have to be taking dance classes. Out of all the extra-curricular activities I was involved in, dance was my jam. I loved learning new routines, and I'll never forget warming up to songs like "Karma Chameleon" by Culture Club and "Everybody Everybody" by Black Box. The best part was the dance recital that involved a sequined costume, some kind of prop, and performing onstage at our local civic center.

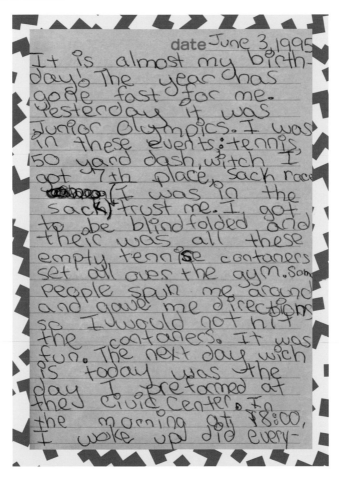

date June 3, 1995

It is almost my birthday. The year has gone fast for me. Yesterday it was Junior Olympics. I was in these events: tennis, 50 yard dash, witch I got 7th place, sack race (I was in the sack) trust me. I got to be blindfolded and their was all these empty tennise contaners set all over the gym. Som people spun me around and gave me directions so I would not hit the contaners. It was fun. The next day wich is today was the day I pretormed at the civic center. In the morning at 8:00, I woke up did every-

Continued on next page

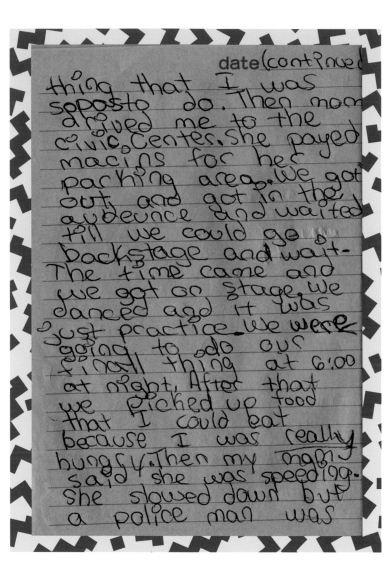

date (continued

thing that I was
soposto do. Then mom
drived me to the
civic Center, she payed
macins for her
parking area. We got
out and got in the
audeince and waited
till we could go
backstage and wait-
The time came and
we got on stage, We
danced and it was
just practice. We were
going to do our
finall thing at 6:00
at night, After that
we picked up food
that I could eat
because I was really
hungry. Then my mom
said she was speeding.
She slowed down but
a police man was

9 years of age
4 grade date (continued)
already pulling her
over. Me and mom were
the only ones in the
car. The police officer was
a guy that lived down
the street. He was really
nice so he didn't give
my mom a ticket for
speeding. Then the officer
let us go, and we started
to go and my moms
hand was on the little
bar and she pushed P,
for park when she
was really should have
done D, for drive. Our car
made a funny sound
and then we went
on. Then my mom got
somthing on her contact
she couldn't get it
out. It was really
scary! I ate, then we
went to a fair at

Continued on next page

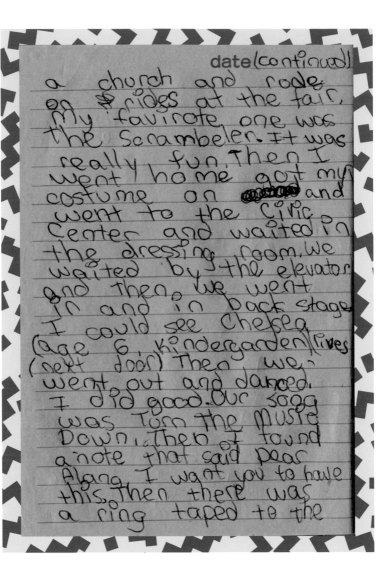

date(continued)

a church and rode on rides at the fair. My favirote one was the Scrambeler. It was really fun. Then I went home got my costume on ~~again~~ and went to the civic center and waited in the dressing room. We waited by the elevator and then we went in and in back stage I could see Chelsea (age 6, kindergarden lives next door) Then we went out and danced. I did good. Our song was Turn the Music Down. Then I found a note that said Dear Alana I want you to have this. Then there was a ring taped to the

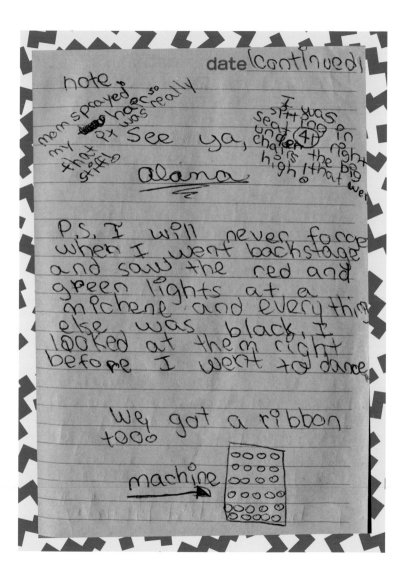

note.

mom sprayed my hair so it was really that stiff. I was really PT See ya,

I was in seat 109 in under chair right that is the big high that was chair

alana

P.S. I will never forge when I went backstage and saw the red and green lights at a michene. and everything else was black. I looked at them right before I went to dance.

we got a ribbon too.

machine

Dance recital outfit, June 6, 1992 (Song: "Black or White" by Michael Jackson).

Dance recital outfit, June 3, 1995 (Song: "Turn the Music Down" by
Gary U. S. Bonds).

FAMILY VACATIONS

I was fortunate enough to have had the opportunity to go on several vacations as a child. Flying was much more expensive back then, so our vacations typically involved a considerable road trip. Instead of flying a couple of hours to Florida, we opted for the sixteen-hour drive that took two full days. Although driving took much longer, it allowed us to visit many places that we most likely would have never seen otherwise. On our trip to Cozumel, Mexico, I seemed to be surprised that most people who lived there were Mexican, and was appalled that a pig was served for dinner with the head still attached.

<u>June 26, 1998</u>

(6)

<u>Dear Journal,</u>

Today my mom woke me up really early. After I got ready, we all went downstairs to eat breakfast. We had a really good meal! All the people here are Mexican but are very nice! :) Anyway, after breakfast, we went up to our hotel room and got our swimming suits on, and our masks, flippers, ect. and went snorkeling in the ocean. We had the <u>best time!!</u> It was soooo oooooo fun because we saw some really pretty fish, and got really close to them. After snorkeling for a little while, we got out to eat lunch. I ate a club sandwitch. It was good! Then we took a taxi into the city and shopped at some stores there and went to Planet Hollywood. We ate dinner there and also bought some shirts. Today I got really sunburnt! :(After we got back to the hotel, It was already dark

Continued on next page

(7)

outside, but the pools ~~were~~ were still open, so me, my mom, and my brother all went swimming. The pool had lights in it so it was fun! Then we came back and I got all my stuff unpacked, and now I'm going to bed.

Goodnight!

Alana

I ♥ Cozumel!

June 27, 1998

8

Dear Journal,

Today I woke up at 9:00 a.m. and got ready for the day. We went down to eat some breakfast at the same buffet we always eat at. After breakfast, we got our snorkel stuff ready and went snorkeling until lunchtime. We ate lunch at the same restaraunt. I had a tropical fruit salad. It was really good! It also came with a little bowl of lemon/lime sherbert. Yum Yum! Then we went swimming in one of the 5 pools at our hotel. After that we could do whatever we wanted. I chose to go snorkeling with my dad and also collect shells. Then we got out of the ocean, and my family and I went up to our hotel and got all dressed up because at 7:30 we are going to a Carribbean party out on the beach. I wore a strawberry dress.

Continued on next page

⑨

When it was time to leave for the party, I was a little nervous, because I had no idea what it would be like. Anyway, when we got to the beach, there was loud music playing. We had to be seated at a big table that could fit about 2 families at it. They did it that way so that we could meet new people. We met a family of 4. They turned out to be really nice! We waited for a long time and finally the buffet opened. As we went through the line and looked at all the food, there was nothing american almost. I had never even seen that kind of food before! and when I got down to the end of the table, there was this huge pig! It was cooked of course, but it had an apple shoved into it's mouth. It looked so scary because it had no eyes, and I looked in it's mouth, and saw a bunch of big sharp teeth!

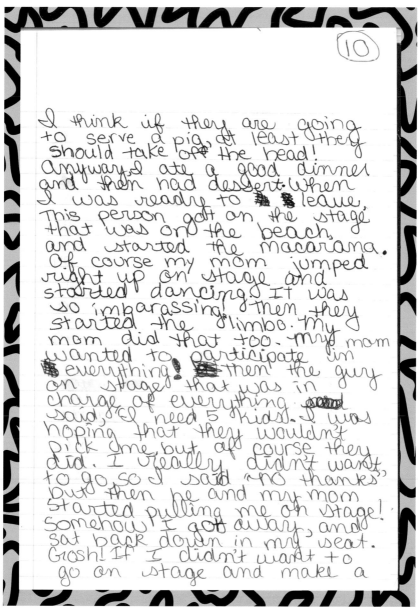

(10)

I think if they are going to serve a pig, at least they should take off the head! Anyway, I ate a good dinner and then had dessert. When I was ready to leave, This person got on the stage that was on the beach, and started the macarana. Of course my mom jumped right up on stage and started dancing. It was so imbarassing! then they started the limbo. My mom did that too. My mom wanted to participate in everything! then the guy on stage that was in charge of everything said, "I need 5 kids. I was hoping that they wouldn't pick me, but of course they did. I really didn't want to go, so I said "no thanks", but then he and my mom started pulling me on stage! Somehow I got away, and sat back down in my seat. Gosh! If I didn't want to go on stage and make a

Continued on next page

⑪

fool out of myself, they shouldn't have forced me to! Then this group of Mexican people got on stage and did kind of a young folk kind of dance thing. They were very good! ☺ Then one of the girls stepped down off the stage and needed a partner to dance with and you can guess who she picked. My dad. Gosh! They can choose out of lots of people because about 5 dozen people went to this party but of course they had to pick people from our family. Anyway my dad looked really funny on stage! He cannot dance!!! The dancing went on till about 10:30 and then the party was over and we all went home. My brother and I went swimming at 10:45 at night. It was cool because the pool lit up. I had a late night tonight! Goodnight!

alana

Fun Things I Found from the Nineties

Mood Ring.

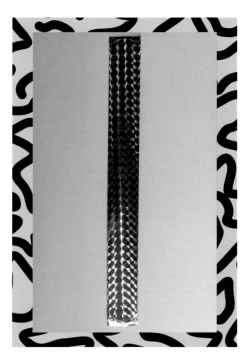

Snap Bracelet.

All of my disgusting baby teeth.

Troll doll.

My absolute favorite books to read were Christopher Pike murder mysteries and the Fear Street series by R. L. Stine.

Denim and plaid purse.

Choker.

Barbie Fold 'n Fun House.

Eighth grade poms uniform.

Who can forget Polly Pockets?

Romper.

Puppy Palace.

Today my prints are everywhere
No matter where you look,
But someday when I am far from home,
you'll 'want them in this book.

About the Author

Although she has been documenting her life in a diary for the past twenty years, Alana Hitchell is a new author and creator of the WordPress blog *My 20-Year Diary*. She holds a BS from Illinois State University with a major in psychology and minor in criminal justice. When she isn't reading books or writing in her diary, she enjoys watching Dateline murder mysteries. Alana still has an extremely unhealthy diet and currently resides in Central Illinois with her boyfriend and beloved dachshund.

Acknowledgments

First and foremost, I'd like to thank my wonderful boyfriend, Jeremy Gonigam. Even though I'm sure he thought the idea of me writing a book sounded a little crazy at first, he never once doubted me and was continually supportive. He experienced all the ups and downs of this process right along with me and was always there if I needed someone to talk to.

I'd like to thank my parents, who worked incredibly hard to provide my siblings and me with such an amazing childhood. A huge thank you to my mom and sister for their support and advice. My sister, Amanda, stayed on the phone with me for hours at times when I needed some direction. I cannot thank her enough for her guidance. I'd also like to thank my Grandma Day, for her continual love and support.

I'd like to thank my friend, Erin Johnson, who was at work with me when I received the news about my book deal. Not only did she allow me a half an hour to go cry in my car, she was also there to share in my joy and excitement.

I'd like to thank my editors, Nicole Mele and Nicole Frail-Magda, for their help in creating this book. I cannot thank them enough for believing in this project and making one of my biggest dreams come true.

I'd also like to thank David Moye from the *Huffington Post* who provided me with advice and encouragement right from the start.

I want to thank Dave Nadelberg for creating *Mortified Nation*, which inspired me to begin blogging and, ultimately, write this book.

I would also like to thank my absolutely amazing sixth grade teacher, Ellen Groesch. When looking through my school papers, I was astonished at the amount of time she took when grading. She always provided helpful feedback, encouragement, and even offered after-school assistance. I am extremely grateful to have had her as my teacher.

I would like to thank the readers of my blog who have been supportive from the very beginning. After two years, I have yet to receive a negative comment. Without them, this book would have not been possible.